OLD FAVORITE
HONEY RECIPES

OLD FAVORITE
HONEY RECIPES

HISTORICAL IMAGES
FAIRVIEW, NORTH CAROLINA

The two earlier works which comprise *Old Favorite Honey Recipes* were products of the American Honey Institute and the Iowa Honey Producers Association

Historical Images
206 Riva Ridge Drive
Fairview, North Carolina 28730

Printed in the United States of America

ISBN-10: 0-914875-55-8
ISBN-13: 978-0-914875-55-0

1941 *Old Favorite Honey Recipes.* 1945 expanded. 1971 *The Honey Recipe Book.*
1991 Books combined to create *Old Favorite Honey Recipes* ISBN: 0-916638-17-0

Cover illustration by Clarence Meyer

Library of Congress Cataloging-in-Publication Data

Old favorite honey recipes.
   p. cm.
  Previously published: Glenwood, Ill. : Meyerbooks, under title: American Honey Institute's old favorite honey recipes and the Honey recipes book of the Iowa Honey Producers Association, 1988.
  "The two earlier works which comprise Old Favorite Honey Recipes were products of the American Honey Institute and the Iowa Honey Producers Association."
  Includes index.
  ISBN-13: 978-0-914875-55-0 (pbk. : alk. paper)
  ISBN-10: 0-914875-55-8 (pbk. : alk. paper)
  1. Cookery (Honey) I. American Honey Institute. II. Iowa Honey Producers Association. III. American Honey Institute's old favorite honey recipes and the Honey recipes book of the Iowa Honey Producers Association.
  TX767.H7A45 2010
  641.6'8--dc22
                  2009039655

CONTENTS

INTRODUCTION

First published in 1941 by the American Honey Institute, *Old Favorite Honey Recipes* was expanded in 1945 and reprinted several times between 1958 and 1977. The Iowa Honey Producers introduced *The Honey Recipe Book* in 1971. Meyerbooks combined the two popular cookbooks into one handy volume in 1991 and published it under the title *Old Favorite Honey Recipes*. With this 2009 edition, Historical Images is pleased to see this popular classic back in the hands of American cooks.

The "two-books-in-one" format of the Meyerbooks edition remains, resulting in some duplication of recipes. The book has been redesigned typographically to allow measurements to be standardized and to eliminate duplication of honey facts and hints for its use. Such material has been gathered from both books into this introduction, omitting irrelevant or out-of-date material and adding notes to update some ingredients or preparation methods.

IMPORTANT HEALTH NOTE

All references to honey as food for infants have been removed. Honey is not recommended for children under one year of age, due to the rare but dangerous possibility of infant botulism.

Also, recipes that contain uncooked eggs in the finished product are still included. However, due to the dangers of Salmonella contamination, using safe egg products, such as eggs pasturized in the shell or powdered pasturized egg whites, is recommended.

Honey Facts and Hints

The sweet taste of honey has made it one of the most enjoyable staples of the human diet for centuries. As evidenced in cave paintings and in the stories and art of ancient peoples, we have loved bees and honey for a long time. While it is hard to imagine a diet without honey, that is exactly how the American colonists lived in the early 1600s. Not native to North America, honeybees had to be imported from England to add a little sweetness to a very hard life. As America has gone through cycles of "getting back to nature," honey has seen surges in popularity. Today, as we see more emphasis on using local resources, honey recipes are back in demand.

Honey's medicinal benefits have been touted for hundreds of years, and new benefits are frequently cited. When ordinary sugars like cane or beet are consumed, they must be broken down by digestive juices before they can be absorbed into the bloodstream and assimilated by the tissues. With honey, little digestion is necessary, so absorption and the resulting energy boost occur quickly. Sugars make up 75 to 80 percent of honey and provide more carbohydrate than the same measure of cane sugar. Besides being an excellent energy food, honey mixed with lemon juice is an effective cough remedy; tea sweetened with honey can sooth a sore throat; and many experts claim that honey has antiseptic properties that aid in healing skin abrasions or minor wounds.

There are a number of types of honey on the market today—liquid, comb, and whipped—as well as numerous flavors named for the flowers from which the bees gather nectar. In addition to the well-known clover honey, one can find such special types as tupelo, orange blossom, and sourwood honeys. Producers frequently mix several honeys to develop a blend with a pleasing flavor.

The ability of honey to absorb and retain moisture means that honey-sweetened breads, cakes, and cookies have excellent keeping qualities. In fact, baked goods sweetened with honey often have a better flavor if kept until the day after baking before serving.

Honey has a long shelf life. For maintaining best quality and for ease in working with honey, consider these hints:

- Freezing does not injure the color or flavor but may hasten granulation.
- Keep honey in a dry place because it has the property of absorbing and retaining moisture.
- Measure shortening or oil before honey using the same measuring cup or spoon and the honey will slide out easily.
- Moisten the measuring spoon or cup first with water or oil before measuring honey to eliminate sticking.
- Store honey covered at room temperature, not in the refrigerator.
- To liquefy honey that has granulated or solidified, place the container in a bowl of warm—not hot—water until all crystals are melted.

🐝　🐝　🐝

The recipes in this collection have been tested only by time and not in a modern kitchen: microwaves and food processors were not in use when these recipes became favorites! Your own experience will no doubt suggest ways to use modern appliances to achieve the same results. Two ingredients often used in times past but less so today are sour milk and fresh (cake or compressed) yeast.

When sour milk is listed, consider the following substitutions:

- Put 1 tablespoon of vinegar or lemon juice in a measuring cup and fill with regular milk to make 1 cup of sour milk; let stand for a few minutes to curdle.
- Use an equal amount of buttermilk.
- Use an equal mix of plain yogurt and water in the required amount.

When fresh yeast is called for, active dry yeast may be substituted. Consult the equivalency notice on the jar or packet. In general:

- One ¼-ounce packet of active dry yeast is equal in activity to one 0.6-ounce cake of yeast.

- A packet contains a scant tablespoonful of yeast and will raise 4 cups, or about 1 pound, of white flour.

- Three ¼-ounce packets of yeast are equal in activity to one 2-ounce cake of yeast.

- Whole wheat and other low-gluten flours require more yeast than white flours.

A few minor adjustments have been made in the recipes to accommodate the modern cook and kitchen:

- Flour is assumed to be white all-purpose unless stated otherwise.

- Honey is assumed to be liquid unless specified otherwise.

- Lard has been replaced by vegetable shortening or vegetable oil.

- For many ingredients, pounds have been converted to cups.

- Oatmeal as an ingredient now reads rolled or quick-cooking oats.

- Oiled paper has been replaced by waxed paper.

- Oven temperatures are given in degrees Fahrenheit.

≈ ≈ ≈

In addition to using recipes in this book, you may choose to adapt some of your own recipes by substituting honey for sugar. Keep these guidelines in mind:

- Cakes made from a mix will be more tender and less crumbly if you add 2 tablespoons of honey in a fine stream to the batter as you beat.

- Remember that honey is a liquid. You may have to add more flour or reduce the amount of other liquid in a recipe to get the proper consistency in the final product. Typically, reduce the amount of liquid ¼ cup for each cup of honey used to replace sugar.

- Use honey in half the amount of sugar called for; that is, if a cup of sugar is listed, a half cup of honey will provide the same degree of sweetening.

- When substituting honey for sugar in a cake, bread, or cookie recipe, lower the oven temperature by about 25° to prevent over-browning.

Book One

OLD FAVORITE
HONEY RECIPES

BEVERAGES

*"A drink that tastes of honey sweet
Will always make a gracious treat."*

Refreshing Party Drink

1 quart currants
2 cups water
1 cup honey
1 small stick cinnamon
Juice of 5 oranges
Juice of 3 lemons
Water for simmering

Wash currants; reserve ¼ cup for garnishing. Place remainder in a saucepan and cover with water. Simmer gently for 10 minutes.

Strain. If a clear juice is desired, do not press the pulp.

Combine the 2 cups water, honey, and cinnamon stick and boil for 5 minutes to make a syrup. Remove the spice stick.

Combine the juice of the oranges, lemons, and currant juice with the spiced syrup. Dilute to taste. Fresh pineapple or cranberry juice may be used instead of orange and lemon juice. Serve hot or cold.

Honey Eggnog

4–6 egg yolks
¼ cup honey
4 cups milk
Nutmeg

Beat the yolks of eggs until lemon colored. Add honey and mix well. Add milk slowly. Fill glasses. Add a slight grating of nutmeg. Serve at once.

FOR ORANGE EGGNOG:

Replace milk with orange juice. Omit nutmeg.

Honey Cocoa Syrup

1¼ cups cocoa
1 cup sugar
½ teaspoon salt
⅛ teaspoon allspice
⅛ teaspoon cinnamon
1½ cups boiling water
½ cup honey
2 teaspoons vanilla extract

Combine cocoa, sugar, salt, and spices. Add boiling water. Blend. Place over low heat, bring to a boil and boil 5 minutes, stirring constantly. Remove from heat. Cool. Add honey and vanilla.

Store in covered jar in refrigerator until ready to use. Honey gives this syrup an unusual smoothness and a delicious flavor in addition to extra food value.

Yields about 2¼ cups.

To serve: Heat ¼ cup Honey Cocoa Syrup with 2 cups scalded milk over boiling water. Before serving, beat with rotary beater.

Yields 3 servings.

Tea

Scald a china or earthen teapot. Allow 1 teaspoon of tea to each cup of freshly boiled water. Pour boiling water over tea. Allow to steep 3 minutes. Serve at once with honey.

Milk

For extra flavor and nourishment, add 2 tablespoons of honey to a glass of milk. Serve hot or cold.

RUSSIAN TEA

1¼ ounces stick cinnamon
1¼ ounces whole cloves
¾ cup honey
3 oranges, juice of 3 and rind of 1
6 lemons, juice of 6 and rind of 1
⅓ cup black tea
5 quarts water, boiling

Grate rinds of orange and lemon.

Cook spices, honey, and grated rind with 2 cups water for 10 minutes. Let stand 1 hour. Strain.

Steep tea in the boiling water 1 minute. Then add fruit juice and spice mixture. Serve hot.

LEMONADE

Mix 2 tablespoons of honey with the juice of half a lemon. Stir well. Add 1 cup hot or cold water according to whether hot or cold drink is desired.

GRAPE JUICE

Mix 2 tablespoons honey with ¼ cup of boiling water. Stir until dissolved. Add enough hot grape juice to fill glass. Two tablespoons of lemon juice may be added for variety. This makes a delicious cold-weather drink.

COFFEE

(medium strong)
2 level tablespoons coffee
1 cup boiling water
(strong)
3 level tablespoons coffee
1 cup boiling water

Put the coffee into the pot with a little egg white or a crushed egg shell. Add a little cold water and stir all together thoroughly.

Measure boiling water and add to the coffee. Place over the heat for 3 minutes. Turn off heat and let settle. Serve with honey.

BREADS

"If I had all of Croesus' money
I'd still subsist on bread and honey."

ENRICHED BREAD

2 cups milk or 1 cup milk and 1 cup
  water
1 tablespoon salt
2 tablespoons shortening
2 tablespoons honey
1 cake compressed or 1 packet dry
  granular yeast
6 cups flour (about)

Scald milk and cool to lukewarm. Add
salt and shortening.

Put honey and yeast in a large mixing
bowl; let stand until yeast is softened.
Add milk and half the flour. Beat thoroughly. Gradually add enough flour to
make a soft dough.

Turn out on floured board and knead
until smooth and elastic (about 8 minutes). Place in lightly greased bowl and
let rise until double in bulk. Punch
down lightly and let rise again. Form
into 2 loaves. Place in greased pans.
Allow to rise until double in bulk.

Bake 40 minutes at 400–425°.

WHOLE WHEAT BREAD

2 cups milk or 1 cup milk and 1 cup
  water
1 tablespoon salt
¼ cup shortening
¼ cup honey
1 cake compressed or 1 packet dry
  granular yeast
5½ cups whole wheat flour (about)

Scald milk and cool to lukewarm. Add
salt, water, and shortening.

Put honey and yeast in a large mixing
bowl; let stand until yeast is softened.
Add the milk mixture and 2 cups
whole wheat flour. Beat thoroughly.
Add another cup of flour and beat
again. Add remainder of flour.

Turn out on floured board and knead
until no longer sticky (about 8 minutes). Place in lightly greased bowl and
let rise until double in bulk. Punch
down and let rise again. Shape into 2
loaves and place in greased pans. Let
rise until double in bulk. Keep dough
at even temperature (85°) for rising.

Bake at 375° for about 50 minutes or
until nicely browned and loaf begins
to shrink from the pan.

ORANGE-NUT BREAD

2 tablespoons shortening
1 cup honey
1 egg
1½ tablespoons grated orange rind
¾ cup orange juice
2¼ cups flour
2½ teaspoons baking powder
⅛ teaspoon baking soda
½ teaspoon salt
¾ cup chopped nuts

Cream the shortening and honey
well. Add the beaten egg and orange
rind. Sift the dry ingredients and add
alternately with the orange juice. Add
chopped nuts. Pour into greased loaf
pan, the bottom of which has been
lined with parchment paper.

Bake at 325° for 1 hour or until the
loaf is nicely browned and begins to
shrink from the pan. Yields 1 loaf.

HONEY OATMEAL BREAD

1½ cups milk
1 cup quick-cooking oats
2 tablespoons shortening
1 can evaporated milk (13-ounce size)
¼ cup honey
1 tablespoon salt
1 or 2 cakes compressed or packets dry
  granular yeast
2 cups white flour
3 cups whole wheat flour (about)

Boil milk, add oats, and cook 2 minutes. Add shortening. When melted, add evaporated milk, honey, and salt. Cool to lukewarm (98°).

Add crumbled yeast and let stand 2 minutes. Add flour and beat well. Add whole wheat flour to form a soft dough. Knead until mixture is smooth (about 8 minutes). Let rise until double in bulk, form into 3 loaves. Let loaves rise until double in bulk.

Bake at 375° for 45–50 minutes.

NUT BREAD

½ cup shortening
½ cup sugar
½ cup honey
1 egg
3 cups sifted flour
3 teaspoons baking powder
1 teaspoon salt
¾ cup milk
1 cup chopped nuts

Cream together shortening and sugar. Add honey and mix thoroughly. Add egg, beating well.

Sift together flour, baking powder, and salt. Add to creamed mixture alternately with milk. Add nuts.

Bake in greased loaf pan at 350° for 1¼ hours. Yields 1 loaf.

WAFFLES

2 cups flour
3 teaspoons baking powder
½ teaspoon salt
1½ cups milk
2 tablespoons plus 1 cup honey
2 eggs, separated and whites beaten
½ cup melted shortening
2–4 tablespoons butter
¼ teaspoon cinnamon

Sift dry ingredients into a medium bowl. In a separate bowl, combine milk, 2 tablespoons honey, egg yolks, shortening, and add to dry ingredients. Fold in stiffly beaten egg whites. Bake in hot waffle iron.

For syrup, heat 1 cup honey in top of double boiler. Add butter and cinnamon, if desired. Serve warm.

HONEY MILK TOAST

2 cups hot milk
½ teaspoon salt
1 tablespoon butter
6 slices buttered toast

Spread each slice of buttered hot toast with honey. Heat milk just to the boiling point, add salt and butter. Keep hot until ready to serve and then pour over the honey-spread toast. Serve at once before toast loses its crispness.

HONEY FRENCH TOAST

2 eggs
2 cups milk
¼ cup honey
½ teaspoon salt
Sprinkling of mace or nutmeg
6 or 8 slices of bread, several days old

Beat eggs until light. Warm the milk slightly and blend well with the honey. Add the salt, mace, and beaten eggs and stir well.

Dip each slice into the milk and egg mixture and place on a hot, well-greased griddle. Brown well on both sides. Serve with honey.

HONEY CINNAMON TOAST

Toast slices of bread on 1 side. While still hot, butter the untoasted side of bread. Spread buttered side with honey. Sprinkle cinnamon over the top. Place slices under broiler until the bread is well browned and the topping is well blended.

REFRIGERATOR ROLLS

½ cup honey
1 cake compressed or 1 packet dry
   granular yeast
½ cup mashed potatoes
2 cups milk (or combination of milk
   and potato water)
1 tablespoon salt
5 cups flour (about)
½ cup melted shortening

Combine honey and yeast and let stand to soften yeast.

Scald milk mixture and add mashed potatoes. Cool to lukewarm.

Combine yeast and liquid mixture. Add salt and half the flour and beat thoroughly. Add melted shortening and remainder of flour to make a soft dough. Knead. Let rise until double in bulk. Punch down and put in a cold place for 24 hours or more, or shape at once and put in a warm place to rise.

Bake at 425° for 15–20 minutes.

Note: If dough in refrigerator rises, punch down. This dough will keep 4–5 days. Put 3 small balls of dough in greased muffin pans for cloverleaf rolls.

PECAN ROLLS

½ cup butter or margarine
1 cup honey
1 cup pecan halves
Sweet roll dough (page 16)

When sweet dough is light, punch down and let rest a few minutes. Roll out in sheet ½″ thick. Brush with butter and spread with honey. Roll as a jelly roll and seal edge firmly. Cut into 1″ slices.

In bottom of the baking pan place butter cut into small pieces. Spread honey over this and scatter with pecans. Place rolls 1″ apart on this mixture. Cover and let rise until double in bulk.

Bake at 375° for 20–25 minutes. Let rolls stand in pans 1 minute after baking before turning them out. If greased muffin pans are used, place 1 teaspoon butter and 1 teaspoon honey in each muffin cup.

SWEET ROLLS

1 cup milk
¼ cup honey
¼ cup shortening
1 teaspoon salt
2 cakes compressed or 2 packets dry
    granular yeast
¼ cup lukewarm water
2 eggs
5 cups flour (about)

Soften yeast in lukewarm water.

Scald milk and place in a large bowl. Add honey, shortening, salt, and softened yeast. Add beaten eggs and half the flour. Beat well. Add rest of flour. Mix well. Knead on a lightly floured board until smooth. Place in lightly greased bowl. Cover and let rise until double in bulk. Punch down and form into rolls or a coffee cake. Let rise again.

Bake at 400°–425° for 20–25 minutes.

CORN BREAD

¾ cup cornmeal
1 cup flour
3 teaspoons baking powder
½ teaspoon salt
1 cup milk
¼ cup honey
1 egg
2 tablespoons melted butter

Mix dry ingredients. Add milk, honey, and beaten egg. Add melted butter last.

Bake 25 minutes in a buttered shallow pan at 400°. Serve with honey.

HONEY ROLLS

1 cup milk
¼ cup shortening
½ cup honey
1 cake compressed or 1 packet dry
    granular yeast, softened in ¼ cup
    lukewarm water
1½ teaspoons salt
4 cups flour
1 egg

Scald milk, place in a large bowl, add shortening and honey, cool to lukewarm. Add yeast, salt, and 2 cups of flour. Add beaten egg and remainder of flour to form a soft dough. Knead lightly until smooth. Let rise twice, then form into rolls. Let rolls rise until light.

Bake at 400° about 20 minutes.

BRAN-RAISIN MUFFINS

1 cup flour
4 teaspoons baking powder
½ teaspoon salt
¾ cup bran
½ cup raisins
½ cup milk
¼ cup honey
2 tablespoons shortening, melted
1 egg, beaten

Sift flour, baking powder, and salt together; stir in bran and add raisins. Combine the milk, honey, melted shortening, and beaten egg. Add dry ingredients. Stir just enough to moisten the flour. Pour into greased muffin pans and bake at 425° for 25 minutes.

Honey Muffins with Variations

2 cups flour
1 teaspoon salt
3 teaspoons baking powder
1 cup milk
¼ cup honey
1 egg, beaten
¼ cup melted shortening

Sift flour with salt and baking powder. Mix milk, honey, beaten egg, and melted shortening together. Add to dry ingredients, stirring just long enough to moisten. Fill greased muffin pans half full.

Bake at 400° for 25–30 minutes or until delicately browned.

BLUEBERRY MUFFINS:

Add ½ cup fresh blueberries to sifted dry ingredients.

FRUIT MUFFINS:

Add ½ cup chopped citron and ¼ cup chopped maraschino cherries to batter. Brush muffins lightly with honey before baking.

HONEY MUFFINS:

Put 1 teaspoon finely crystallized honey in center of batter of each muffin.

PEANUT BUTTER MUFFINS:

Blend ¼ cup peanut butter with honey before adding to milk and egg mixture.

SOYBEAN MUFFINS:

Replace ½ cup flour with ½ cup soybean flour.

WHOLE WHEAT MUFFINS:

Replace 1 cup of flour with 1 cup of whole wheat flour.

Honey Currant Cake

1 cake compressed or 1 packet dry
   granular yeast, softened in ¼ cup
   lukewarm water
½ cup milk
¼ cup honey
1 teaspoon salt
¼ cup melted shortening
1 egg
2 cups sifted enriched flour (about)
½ cup currants
¼ cup honey
¼ teaspoon cinnamon
¼ cup chopped nuts

Scald milk and cool to lukewarm. Add honey, salt, and shortening. Beat egg and add. Blend thoroughly. Add 1 cup flour and beat well. Add softened yeast. Add currants and remaining flour to make a moderately stiff drop batter. Beat until smooth. Cover and let rise until bubbly (about 1 hour).

Stir down, pour into greased 8″ x 8″ 2″ pan, filling pan about half full. Spread batter with honey. Sprinkle cinnamon and chopped nuts over honey. Let rise until double in bulk.

Bake at 375° for 35–40 minutes. Yields 1 cake.

Note: May also be baked as muffins, 20–25 minutes. Yields 1½ dozen 2″ muffins.

CORN MUFFINS

¾ cup sifted flour
1¼ teaspoons baking powder
½ teaspoon salt
⅓ cup cornmeal
¼ cup prepared apple
1 egg, well beaten
⅓ cup milk
¼ cup honey
3 tablespoons shortening, melted

Sift flour once, measure, add baking powder and salt, and sift again. Add cornmeal. Wash, pare, and cut apples into eighths. Remove core and cut apple crosswise into very thin slices. Combine egg, milk, honey, and shortening. Add all at once to the flour/cornmeal mixture, stirring only enough to dampen. Fold in apple.

Bake in well-greased 2″ muffin pans at 400° for 20 minutes or until done. Yields 8–12 muffins.

HONEY ORANGE MUFFINS

½ cup sifted flour
½ teaspoon salt
2 teaspoons baking powder
½ cup whole wheat flour
1 egg, well beaten
¼ cup orange juice
1 teaspoon grated orange rind
½ cup honey
3 tablespoons melted shortening

Sift flour, salt, and baking powder together. Add whole wheat flour and mix thoroughly. In another bowl, combine egg, orange juice and rind, honey, and shortening. Add all at once to flour, stirring only enough to dampen.

Bake in well-greased muffin pans at 400° for 15–20 minutes or until browned.

QUICK COFFEE CAKE WITH HONEY TOPPING

1½ cups sifted flour
2 teaspoons baking powder
½ teaspoon salt
1 egg
⅔ cup milk
⅓ cup honey
3 tablespoons melted shortening

Sift together dry ingredients into a medium bowl.

In a separate bowl, beat egg and add milk, honey, and melted shortening. Stir into dry ingredients. Mix lightly (only enough to moisten flour). Spread in lightly greased 8″ square pan. Cover batter with Honey Topping.

Bake at 400° for 25–30 minutes.

HONEY TOPPING:

¼ cup butter or margarine
¼ cup sugar
¼ cup sifted flour
¼ cup honey
¼ cup chopped nuts

Cream butter or margarine. Add sugar, flour, and honey and mix thoroughly. Spread over batter and then sprinkle with nuts.

CAKES

"With butter, egg, and good honey
Your cake will moist and flaky be."

HONEY ANGEL FOOD CAKE

1 teaspoon cream of tartar
½ teaspoon salt
1 cup egg whites (8–10 whites)
¾ cup sugar
1 cup cake flour
½ cup honey
½ teaspoon grated lemon rind

Add the cream of tartar and salt to the egg whites in a bowl. Beat the whites with a wire whip until they are stiff. They should move only slightly when the bowl is tipped. Fold half the sugar slowly into the egg whites 2 tablespoons at a time. Sift the remaining sugar with the flour for later.

The ½ cup honey must be warmed so that it will be thin and will pour in a fine stream over the egg whites as the egg whites are folded in.

After the honey is added, fold in the flour and sugar mixture, sifting ¼ cup over the whites at a time. Add grated lemon rind. Pour the mixture into an ungreased angel food pan.

Bake at 300° for 50 minutes. Invert the pan, cool, and remove to a cake rack.

UNCOOKED HONEY FROSTING

⅛ teaspoon salt
1 egg white
½ cup honey
½ teaspoon flavoring

Add salt to egg white. Warm honey over hot water. Pour in a thin stream over egg white while beating vigorously. Add flavoring. Continue to beat until thick and fluffy.

CHOCOLATE HONEY ANGEL FOOD CAKE

¾ cup sifted cake flour
¼ cup cocoa
1 cup sifted granulated sugar
1 cup egg whites (8–10 whites)
¼ teaspoon salt
¾ teaspoon cream of tartar
1 teaspoon vanilla extract
⅓ cup honey

Sift flour once, measure, add cocoa and ¼ cup of the sugar, and sift together 4 times.

Beat egg whites and salt with rotary beater or flat wire whisk. When foamy, add cream of tartar and vanilla. Continue beating until eggs are stiff enough to peak but not dry. Add remaining ¾ cup of sugar, 2 tablespoons at a time, beating after each addition until sugar is just blended. Add honey, 2 tablespoons at a time, beating after each addition until honey is just blended.

Sift about ¼ cup flour/sugar mixture over egg whites and fold in lightly; repeat until all flour is used. Turn into ungreased angel food pan. Cut gently through batter with knife to remove air bubbles.

Bake at 325° for 1 hour. Remove from oven and invert pan 1 hour or until cold.

Super Delicious Chocolate Cake

3 squares unsweetened chocolate, melted
2/3 cup honey
1¾ cups sifted cake flour
1 teaspoon baking soda
¾ teaspoon salt
½ cup butter or other shortening
½ cup sugar
1 teaspoon vanilla extract
2 eggs, unbeaten
2/3 cup water

Blend chocolate and honey; cool to lukewarm. Sift flour once, measure, add baking soda and salt, and sift together 3 times. Cream butter thoroughly, add sugar gradually, and cream together until light and fluffy. Add chocolate/honey mixture and vanilla. Blend. Add eggs, one at a time, beating thoroughly after each addition. Add flour, alternately with water, a small amount at a time, beating after each addition until smooth.

Bake in 2 greased 8″ layer pans at 350° for 30–35 minutes. Spread with French Honey Chocolate Frosting.

FRENCH HONEY CHOCOLATE FROSTING:

½ cup sugar
¼ cup butter
¼ cup light cream
¼ cup honey
¼ teaspoon salt
3 squares unsweetened chocolate, cut into small pieces
2 egg yolks, well beaten

Combine sugar, butter, cream, honey, salt, and chocolate in top of double boiler. Place over boiling water. When chocolate is melted, beat with rotary beater until blended. Pour small amount of mixture over egg yolks, stirring vigorously. Return to double boiler and cook 2 minutes longer, or until mixture thickens slightly, stirring constantly. Remove from hot water, place in pan of ice water or cracked ice, and beat until of right consistency to spread. Yields enough frosting to cover tops and sides of two 8″ layers.

Honey Ginger Cake

2½ cups sifted cake flour
1 teaspoon baking soda
½ teaspoon baking powder
1 teaspoon salt
1 teaspoon ground ginger
1 teaspoon cinnamon
½ cup butter
½ cup brown sugar, firmly packed
1 egg, unbeaten
1 cup honey
1 cup buttermilk

Sift flour once and measure. Add baking soda, baking powder, salt, and spices, then sift together 3 times. Cream butter thoroughly, add sugar gradually, and cream together until light and fluffy. Add egg and beat thoroughly. Add honey and blend. Add flour, alternately with buttermilk, a small amount at a time, beating after each addition until smooth.

Bake in 2 well-greased 9″ layer pans at 350° for 45 minutes or until done.

Note: If baked in paper-lined cupcake pans, bake at 350° for 30 minutes.

GOLD CAKE

¼ cup butter or margarine
½ cup honey
1 teaspoon orange extract
1 cup sifted flour
1½ teaspoons baking powder
½ teaspoon salt
4 egg yolks
¼ cup milk

Cream butter or margarine. Add honey gradually and beat well. Add extract. Sift together flour, baking powder, and salt. Add a quarter of the sifted dry ingredients. Add eggs and beat well. Add remaining ingredients.

Bake 40–45 minutes in greased loaf pan at 350°.

HONEY LAYER CAKE

½ cup shortening
½ cup sugar
½ cup honey
2 eggs, separated and whites beaten
2 cups sifted cake flour
3 teaspoons baking powder
¾ teaspoon salt
¾ cup milk
½ teaspoon flavoring

Cream shortening thoroughly. Add sugar and honey, beat until mixture is light and fluffy. Add egg yolks and beat well. Add sifted dry ingredients alternately with milk. Add flavoring and fold in stiffly beaten egg whites.

Bake in 2 layers at 350° for 30 minutes.

Note: Spread lemon, fig, or orange filling between layers (recipes follow). If you desire a Chocolate Flake Cake, fold in with the beaten egg whites 1 cup chocolate flakes made by grating unsweetened chocolate.

LEMON FILLING:

¼ cup sugar
2 tablespoons flour
¼ cup lemon juice
½ cup honey
Grated rind of 1 lemon
1 egg, lightly beaten
1 tablespoon butter

Mix ingredients in top of double boiler. Cook over hot water, stirring constantly until thickened. Cool. Spread between layers of cake.

FIG FILLING:

½ cup chopped figs
½ cup honey
¼ cup water
2 tablespoons orange juice
1 tablespoon cornstarch

Mix ingredients in top of double boiler and cook until thick enough to spread. Spread while hot between cake layers.

ORANGE FILLING:

2 tablespoons sugar
2 tablespoons flour
½ tablespoon lemon juice
½ cup orange juice
¼ cup honey
Grated rind of 1 orange
1 egg, lightly beaten
1 tablespoon butter

Mix ingredients in top of double boiler and cook until thickened. Cool and spread between cake layers.

HONEY FRUITCAKE

2 cups butter or other shortening
1½ cups brown sugar, firmly packed
1 cup honey
9 eggs
4 cups flour
1 teaspoon baking soda
1 teaspoon cinnamon
1 teaspoon mace
3 tablespoons milk
6 cups raisins, lightly floured
6 cups currants, lightly floured
3⅓ cups blanched almonds
2 cups candied citron, diced
2 cups candied orange, diced
2 cups candied lemon, diced
Candied cherries and candied rhubarb
    if desired

Cream butter, add sugar and honey and cream well. Add well-beaten eggs. Sift together flour, baking soda, and spices; add alternately with milk. Add currants, raisins, almonds, and candied fruit. Mix well and place in pans that have been lined with parchment paper.

Decorate top of cake with cherries, almonds, and strips of citron. Place parchment paper over top of cake.

Steam for 2½ hours and then bake at 250° for 2 hours.

HONEY MERINGUE

1 egg white
½ cup honey

Beat egg white until it begins to froth. Add honey, gradually beating until meringue stands high in peaks, (about 5–10 minutes). Use on puddings or cakes.

TUTTI FRUTTI CAKE

1 cup cooked prunes
1¾ cups raisins
½ cup sliced citron
⅓ cup sliced candied lemon peel
½ cup sliced candied orange peel
½ cup sliced candied cherries
2 teaspoons cinnamon
1 teaspoon mace
½ teaspoon cloves
½ teaspoon allspice
1 cup prune juice
½ cup orange juice
1 cup honey
1 cup shortening
1 cup sugar
4 eggs
1 cup chopped walnuts
5 cups sifted flour
1½ teaspoons salt
1¼ teaspoons baking soda

Remove pits and cut prunes into small pieces. Combine fruits and peels with spices, cover with fruit liquids and honey, blend well, and let stand over night.

Cream shortening with sugar, add well-beaten eggs, and combine with fruit mixture and nuts. Add flour sifted with salt and baking soda, and blend thoroughly. Pour into parchment paper-lined tube pan (about 10" x 4").

Bake at 300° for 3–3¼ hours. Before removing from oven, test with cake tester. Makes about a 5-pound cake.

NUT CAKE

½ cup shortening
1 cup sugar
½ cup honey
¾ cup cold water
2 cups sifted cake flour
1 cup nut pieces, lightly floured
4 egg whites, beaten
4 teaspoons baking powder
1 teaspoon lemon extract

Cream shortening and sugar. Add honey. Beat well. Add flour and cold water alternately. Add half the beaten egg whites and nuts. Fold in remainder of beaten egg whites, baking powder, and extract.

Bake in 9″ x 12″ cake pan at 350° for 50–60 minutes. Frost with Uncooked Honey Frosting (page 21).

BOILED HONEY FROSTING

1½ cups honey
⅛ teaspoon salt
2 egg whites

Cook honey and salt to 238° or until it will spin a thread or make a soft ball when dropped into cold water. Beat egg whites. Pour the hot honey in a thin stream over the beaten egg whites, continuing to beat until all honey is added and frosting will stand in peaks. Spread on cake.

CHOPPED APRICOT VARIATION:

Add ⅔ cup of well-washed, chopped dried apricots. Add ¼ teaspoon each of almond and lemon extract. This frosting gives a new flavor to a light cake.

EVERYDAY CAKE

⅓ cup shortening
½ cup sugar
½ cup honey
1 egg
½ cup milk
2 cups sifted cake flour
2 teaspoons baking powder
¼ teaspoon salt
1 teaspoon lemon extract

Cream shortening. Add sugar and cream well. Add honey and beat until light and fluffy. Add egg and beat thoroughly. Add sifted dry ingredients alternately with milk. Add extract.

Bake in 2 layers at 375° for 25–30 minutes. Put layers together with French Honey Chocolate Frosting (page 22).

APPLESAUCE CAKE

⅓ cup shortening
¾ cup honey
2 cups flour
¼ teaspoon cloves
½ teaspoon cinnamon
½ teaspoon nutmeg
¼ teaspoon salt
1 teaspoon baking soda
1 cup cold, unsweetened applesauce
1 cup raisins

Cream shortening. Add honey gradually, creaming after each addition.

Sift dry ingredients together into another bowl. Add alternately with the applesauce to the creamed mixture. Fold in raisins. Pour batter into a well-greased 8″ x 8″ pan.

Bake at 350° for about 45 minutes.

Orange Honey Cake

2 cups sifted cake flour
3½ teaspoons baking powder
¾ teaspoon salt
½ cup butter or other shortening
½ cup sugar
⅔ cup honey
2 egg yolks
2 egg whites, stiffly beaten
½ cup orange juice

Sift flour once, measure, add baking powder and salt, and sift together 3 times. Cream butter thoroughly, add sugar gradually, and cream together until light and fluffy. Add honey. Blend. Add egg yolks and beat thoroughly. Add flour, alternately with orange juice, a small amount at a time, beating after each addition until smooth. Fold in egg whites.

Bake in 2 greased 9″ layer pans at 350° for 30–35 minutes.

Honey Sour Cream Spice Cupcakes

½ cup shortening
1 cup brown sugar, firmly packed
1 cup honey
3 eggs, separated and whites beaten
2 cups flour
¼ teaspoon salt
1 teaspoon ground cloves
1 teaspoon allspice
1 teaspoon cinnamon
1 teaspoon baking soda
1 cup thick sour cream

Cream shortening, add sugar and honey, and cream well again. Add egg yolks one at a time, beating well after each addition.

Sift dry ingredients and add alternately with the sour cream, beating after each addition. Fold in stiffly beaten egg whites.

Bake in greased muffin pans at 350° for 30 minutes, or in a greased cake pan for 40 minutes.

Spice Cake

½ cup shortening
¾ cup honey
2 cups sifted cake flour
2 teaspoons baking powder
½ teaspoon salt
1 teaspoon cinnamon
½ teaspoon cloves
¼ teaspoon nutmeg
2 eggs, separated and whites beaten
½ cup milk
½ cup chopped nuts
½ cup chopped raisins

Cream shortening, add honey, and beat thoroughly.

Mix and sift together flour, baking powder, salt, and spices. Add about 1 cup of sifted dry ingredients to shortening and honey mixture. Beat well. Add egg yolks and beat. Add remaining dry ingredients alternately with milk. Add nuts and raisins with last addition of flour. Fold in stiffly beaten egg whites. Pour batter into greased tube pan.

Bake at 350° for 60 minutes, or until done.

GINGERBREAD

2 cups sifted flour
2 teaspoons baking powder
1 teaspoon salt
½ teaspoon ground ginger
½ teaspoon ground cloves
½ teaspoon nutmeg
½ cup shortening
⅓ cup sugar
½ cup honey
2 eggs, lightly beaten
¾ cup milk

Combine first six ingredients and sift together 3 times. Cream shortening. Add sugar and honey and beat well. Add ½ cup of sifted dry ingredients and mix thoroughly. Add beaten eggs. Add remainder of dry ingredients alternately with milk.

Bake in greased pan at 375° about 35–40 minutes. Cut into squares and top with Honey Meringue (page 24).

LOAF CAKE

⅔ cup shortening
1½ cups honey
3 eggs, well beaten
3 cups flour
3 teaspoons baking powder
½ teaspoon salt
1 teaspoon cinnamon
1 teaspoon mace
½ cup fruit juice
1 cup raisins
1 cup chopped nuts

Cream shortening; add honey gradually. Blend well. Add well-beaten eggs.

Into another bowl, sift dry ingredients together. Add alternately with the fruit juice. Stir in raisins and nuts. Pour into 2 loaf pans lined with parchment paper.

Bake 1 hour at 350°.

CANDIES

"All candy calls for flavor sweet
And honey therein can't be beat."

HONEY TAFFY

2 cups sugar
2 cups honey
⅔ cup cold water
⅛ teaspoon salt

Boil sugar, honey, and water to brittle stage, 288°. Add salt. Put in buttered dish to cool; pull until white.

SPICED HONEY NUTS

3 cups sifted confectioners sugar
3 teaspoons cinnamon
1½ teaspoons nutmeg
1½ teaspoons allspice
1 egg white, unbeaten
2 tablespoons honey
⅛ teaspoon salt
4 cups almonds, pecans, or walnuts

Sift sugar and spices together 3 times. Spread half of the mixture ¼" thick on baking sheet or shallow pan. Place egg white, honey, and salt in bowl and beat until mixed but not foamy. Add nuts and stir until coated. Place nuts on sugar mixture, one at a time, top side up, ¼" apart. Cover evenly with remaining sugar mixture.

Set pan inside another baking sheet, or pan, and bake at 250° for 1½ hours*. Remove nuts immediately and brush off excess sugar. Cool. Store in airtight glass jar. Yields about 1 pound.

* A very low oven is necessary to make nuts crisp and to prevent them from becoming too brown.

HONEY CHOCOLATE FUDGE

2 cups sugar
1 square unsweetened chocolate
¼ teaspoon salt
1 cup evaporated milk
¼ cup honey
2 tablespoons butter
1 cup chopped nuts

Boil sugar, chocolate, salt, and milk for five minutes. Add honey and cook to soft-ball stage, 240°. Add butter; let stand until lukewarm; beat until creamy, add nuts, and pour into buttered pan. Cut when firm.

HONEY FONDANT

⅔ cup honey
4 cups sugar
2 cups boiling water

Cook honey, sugar, and water slowly. Do not let boil until sugar is dissolved. Keep crystals off side of the pan with a cold wet cloth wrapped around a fork. When sugar is dissolved, bring to a boil and boil slowly to the soft-ball stage, 238°. Keeping a cover on the pan part of the time helps to keep the crystals from forming. Flavoring, if desired, may be added at this point. Remove from heat and pour at once on large buttered platters.

When lukewarm, stir until creamy. Knead until smooth. Fondant improves if allowed to stand a few days before using. Flavor as desired.

HONEYED FRUIT STRIPS

Orange peel
Water
Salt
Honey

Remove peel from 3 oranges; cut peel into strips. Cover with water to which 1 teaspoon of salt has been added. Boil 30 minutes, drain, cover with fresh water, boil again until peel is tender. Drain. Add enough honey to cover, from ¾–1 cup. Let simmer very slowly until peel is clear (about 45 minutes). Lay on waxed paper and let stand 2–3 days before using.

VARIATIONS:

Grapefruit peel and lemon peel may be similarly prepared.

Fruit strips may be rolled in coconut or nuts and used as a confection.

Peel may be coated with confectioners chocolate.

Peel may be chopped and used in cookies, nut bread, or muffin mixtures.

HONEY POPCORN BALLS

¾ cup sugar
1 teaspoon salt
½ cup water
¾ cup honey
3 quarts popcorn

Cook sugar, salt, and water (stir until sugar is dissolved) to very brittle stage, 300°. Add honey slowly, stirring until blended. Cook again until thermometer registers 240° (about 1 minute). Pour over popcorn and form into balls. Wrap in heavy waxed paper.

HONEY CARAMELS

2 cups sugar
2 cups honey
Few grains of salt
½ cup butter
1 cup evaporated milk

Cook sugar, honey, and salt rapidly to hard-ball stage, 250°. Stir occasionally. Add butter and milk gradually so the mixture does not stop boiling at any time. Cook rapidly to hard-ball stage, 250°. Stir constantly so mixture will not stick. Pour into buttered pan and cool thoroughly before cutting into squares. Wrap individually in waxed paper.

HONEY DIVINITY

2 cups sugar
⅓ cup honey
⅓ cup water
2 egg whites, beaten
½ cup chopped nuts

Boil sugar, honey, and water until syrup spins a thread (278°). Pour syrup over well-beaten egg whites, beating continuously. Just before mixture starts to set, add chopped nuts. When mixture crystallizes, drop with a spoon on waxed paper.

VARIATION:

Candied cherries or candied rhubarb may be added.

HONEY BITTERSWEETS

Comb honey
Hot water
Confectioners chocolate

Let comb honey remain in refrigerator 24 hours before using. Cut comb honey into pieces about ¾" long and ⅜" wide with knife that is dipped in boiling water. Place pieces on trays covered with waxed paper; chill 30 minutes.

Coat with dipping chocolate. Drop a nut on each piece. (It requires a little practice to be able to turn out honeyed bittersweets that do not develop honey leaks.) It is necessary to have dipping chocolate at proper temperature (about 70°–75°) when coating. Coating in a room of 60°–65° will cause the chocolate to harden more quickly.

HONEY PENUCHE

2 cups brown sugar, firmly packed
¼ teaspoon salt
⅔ cup white sugar
1 cup milk
¼ cup honey
3 tablespoons butter
½ cup chopped nuts

Combine first 5 ingredients and cook over low heat to 240°. Stir just enough to prevent sticking. Remove from heat, add butter, and cool to lukewarm without stirring. Then beat until candy begins to thicken. Add nuts and turn into a greased shallow pan. When firm, cut into squares.

CREAM CANDY

1 cup sugar
¼ cup cream
¼ cup honey
1 tablespoon butter
½ cup chopped nuts

Mix sugar, cream, and honey. Cook until the sugar is dissolved. Add butter and continue without stirring until a very soft-ball stage is reached at 236°. Remove from heat and begin to beat at once. Beat until thick and dull in appearance. Add nuts just before turning out into greased pan. Cut with a warm knife before the mixture is cold.

FRUIT CANDY

¼ cup dried prunes
¼ cup dried apricots
¼ cup dried figs
½ cup dates
¼ cup raisins
⅓ cup honey
Chopped nuts, coconut, or
  confectioners chocolate

Let cleaned dried prunes and apricots stand in boiling water for five minutes. Run all the fruit through a food chopper with fine blade. Add honey. With buttered hands shape into balls. Roll in chopped nuts, coconut, or coat with confectioners chocolate. Nuts may be added and other dried fruits like peaches and pears used.

HONEY TWISTS

½ cup honey
1 cup sugar
½ cup milk
¼ teaspoon salt
1 teaspoon vanilla extract

Combine all ingredients and cook over a low heat until when tested a hard ball is formed in cold water, 260°. Stir occasionally. Pour into a shallow greased pan. Pull until light and firm as soon as it is cool enough to handle. Twist into rope form and cut in 1 or 2" lengths. Wrap in waxed paper and store in a cool place.

HONEY MARSHMALLOWS

1 tablespoon unflavored gelatin
¼ cup cold water
1 cup honey
5 cups shredded coconut

Dissolve gelatin in cold water. Add to the honey which has been heated. Beat until very light and fluffy (about 10 minutes by machine or 20 minutes by hand). Turn out on oiled pan and let stand 24–48 hours. Toast coconut and roll to make fine. Spread coconut over the surface of a large pan and turn the marshmallows on it. Dip knife into cold water and cut into squares. Roll each piece in the coconut.

NOUGAT

¾ cup honey
1 cup sugar
¼ teaspoon salt
½ cup water
2 egg whites, beaten
1 teaspoon flavoring
¾ cup chopped nuts

Combine honey, sugar, salt, and water and cook over low heat. Stir until sugar is dissolved and mixture starts to boil. Boil without stirring to 300°. Pour hot syrup slowly over stiffly beaten egg whites, beating constantly. Fold in nuts and flavoring. Spread in greased square pan. Cool and cut in rectangular pieces.

PEANUT BRITTLE

2 cups sugar
1 cup honey
1 cup water
2 cups salted peanuts
1 tablespoon butter

Put sugar, honey, and water in saucepan. Stir until sugar is dissolved. Cook to 300°. Remove from heat. Add butter and peanuts. Stir just enough to mix thoroughly. Pour into very thin sheets on a well-greased platter. Cool. Break into pieces to serve.

HONEY SQUARES

¼ cup honey
2 cups sugar
3 tablespoons water
¼ teaspoon salt
1 cup chopped nuts
1 teaspoon flavoring

Cook honey, sugar, water, and salt until soft-ball stage is reached. Take from heat. Add nuts and flavoring, beat until creamy, pour on buttered pan, and cut into squares.

SUPER DELICIOUS CARAMELS

1½ cups light cream
2 cups sugar
¼ cup butter
1 cup honey
½ teaspoon vanilla extract
1 cup nuts

Cook first 4 ingredients over low heat to 254°, or hard-ball stage, stirring constantly toward the end of the cooking period. Add vanilla and nuts. Pour into buttered pan. Cut when cold and wrap each in waxed paper.

CANDY ROLL

½ pound sweet chocolate (cooking)
6 tablespoons honey, divided
¼ teaspoon salt
3 teaspoons cold water
1 cup peanut butter

Melt chocolate in top of double boiler over hot (not boiling) water. Add 3 tablespoons honey and salt. Stir until smooth. Add water, about 1 teaspoon at a time, beating well after each addition. Beat until smooth and shiny.

Pour mixture on sheet of waxed paper. Spread into rectangular shape. Let stand for 10–15 minutes.

Blend peanut butter and the remaining 3 tablespoons honey and spread on chocolate. Roll up like jelly roll. Wrap well in waxed paper and place in refrigerator over night. Cut in slices to serve.

CONFITURES

"A little honey in the canning
Mixed with the juices is good planning."

HONEY ORANGE MARMALADE

2 medium oranges
¼ medium grapefruit
⅓ lemon
4¾ cups water per pound of fruit
1⅔ cups sugar per pound of fruit and liquid
⅓ cup honey per pound of fruit and liquid

Cut the fruit into very thin slices, cut each slice into eighths, remove the seeds, the pithy inner portion, and about half of the orange rind. Add the water to the fruit and let stand in the refrigerator 24 hours. Remove. Boil steadily for about 1 hour or until the rind is tender and slightly translucent. Weigh the fruit and liquid and add the required amount of sugar. Boil slowly until it reaches 214°, add the required amount of honey, and cook to 218°. Remove from stove and seal in sterilized glasses. Yields about 1 quart.

RHUBARB JELLY

1 cup rhubarb juice
2 tablespoons granulated pectin
1 cup honey

Wash and cut rhubarb into inch lengths. Place in preserving kettle. Add enough water to prevent it from sticking. Cook slowly in covered kettle until soft. Strain in jelly bag. Measure juice. Add pectin and stir vigorously. Bring to a boil. Add honey and continue to boil until jelly test is secured. Fill hot, sterilized glasses with jelly. Cover with paraffin.

CURRANT JELLY

Pick over currants; do not remove stems. Wash, drain, and place in preserving kettle. Mash with potato masher. Add ½ cup water to about 2 quarts fruit. Bring to a boil and simmer until currants appear transparent. Strain through a jelly bag. Measure juice. Add ¾ cup honey and ¾ cup sugar to 2 cups juice.

Cook only 4 cups of juice at a time. Stir until sugar dissolves. Cook until 2 drops run together and "sheet" off spoon. Fill hot, sterilized glasses. Cover with paraffin.

HONEY CHUTNEY

2 quarts sour apples
2 green peppers
3 medium onions
2¼ cups raisins
½ tablespoon salt
1 cup honey
Juice of 2 lemons and the grated rind of 1
1½ cups vinegar
¾ cup tart fruit juice
¾ tablespoon ground ginger
¼ teaspoon cayenne pepper

Wash and chop fruit and vegetables. Add all other ingredients and simmer until thick like chili sauce. Seal in hot, sterilized jars.

SUNSHINE CHERRY PRESERVES

1½ cups honey
1½ cups sugar
1 quart pitted cherries

Combine honey and sugar, bring slowly to the boiling point, add cherries, and cook 12 minutes. Pour out into shallow dishes, cover with glass, and allow to stand in the sunshine 1 day or longer. Seal in hot, sterilized jars.

SWEET APPLE PICKLES

2 cups honey
1 cup vinegar
2 inches stick cinnamon
6 whole cloves
Apples

Combine honey, vinegar, and spices, and heat to boiling. Have ready 8–10 cups of quartered apples (pared or not, as you like). Cook 2–3 cups of apples at a time in the syrup, handling them gently so they will not mash. When transparent, lift out, place in a jar or bowl, and continue until all are cooked. Take out spices, pour remaining syrup over the apples, and store in sterilized jars until needed. Serve cold with meats.

CANNED PEACHES

3 cups water
½ cup sugar
½ cup honey
12 peaches

Prepare syrup by boiling water and sugar for 5 minutes. Add honey. Scald peaches in boiling water to loosen skins, peel, cut in halves, and remove stones. Retain 2 peach stones. Cook fruit with 2 peach stones in syrup. Cook 5–10 minutes. Test by piercing with silver fork. Arrange peaches when done with cut side down in jar. Fill to overflowing with hot syrup and remove air bubbles with sterilized knife. Cover with lid just taken from boiling water.

Note: Pears may be canned in the same way.

COOKIES

*"Of all the cookies I have eaten
Those made with honey can't be beaten."*

EVERYDAY COOKIES

½ cup shortening
½ cup sugar
½ cup honey
1 egg, well beaten
⅔ cup flour
½ teaspoon baking soda
½ teaspoon baking powder
¼ teaspoon salt
1 cup quick-cooking oats
1 cup shredded coconut
1 teaspoon vanilla extract
½ cup chopped nuts

Cream shortening, sugar, and honey together until light and fluffy. Add well-beaten egg and blend. Sift flour with dry ingredients and stir into batter. Add oats, coconut, vanilla, and nuts. Spread on greased baking sheets and bake at 350° for 12–15 minutes. Cut into bars.

HONEY PECAN COOKIES

½ cup shortening
1 cup honey
1 egg
¼ cup sour milk
2 cups flour
½ teaspoon baking soda
½ teaspoon salt
¾ cup pecans
¾ cup each of raisins, cherries, and
    dates

Cream shortening and honey, add the egg, sour milk, and flour, which has been sifted with baking soda and salt. Add the nuts and fruit. Drop on greased pans and bake at 350° for 15 minutes.

BUTTER COOKIES

2 cups butter
1 cup honey
2 eggs, separated
Grated rind of ½ lemon
8 cups flour
1¼ teaspoons baking powder
Juice of ½ lemon
1 cup almonds, chopped

Cream butter; add honey, lightly beaten egg yolks; add grated lemon rind and flour mixed with baking powder. Add lemon juice. Chill dough. The dough may be formed into small balls or rolled out and cut in shapes. Brush with the egg white and sprinkle the chopped almonds on top. Bake at 350° for 10–15 minutes. (Will keep well.)

VARIATIONS:

Divide dough into 8 parts. Using food coloring, color first part red, second part blue, third part green, fourth part yellow. Add ½ ounce melted chocolate to fifth part. Keep sixth part natural color. Add ¼ teaspoon cinnamon, ¼ teaspoon nutmeg to seventh part, and any combination of fruit (dates or raisins) and chopped nuts to the eighth part.

Many different shapes and combinations will suggest themselves; for example, roll red dough ⅛" thick into a rectangle, roll the green the same thickness and size. Place on top of red. Roll as for a jelly roll. Chill, cut into thin slices. Bake as above.

RAISIN HONEY GEMS

1½ cups honey
¾ cup shortening
1 egg, beaten
2½ cups flour
¼ teaspoon salt
¼ teaspoon baking soda
2¼ teaspoons baking powder
1 teaspoon cinnamon
1½ cups rolled oats
¾ cup raisins
2 tablespoons hot water

Cream honey and shortening. Add beaten egg. Sift flour, salt, baking soda, baking powder, and cinnamon into mixture. Add oats, raisins, and water. Mix thoroughly. Drop by teaspoon upon greased cookie sheet. Bake at 375° for 15 minutes.

HONEY CAKES

4 cups honey
3⅓ cups sugar
2½ pounds flour
1 cup citron
1 tablespoon cinnamon
1 tablespoon cloves
1 teaspoon cardamom
1 nutmeg, grated
7 eggs
1 pound flour
1¼ pounds almonds
2 lemons, juice and grated rind
1 teaspoon baking powder (optional)

Should be made a month before using.

Heat honey and sugar together over low heat until sugar is dissolved. Add the 2½ pounds of flour. Remove from heat. Add the citron, cut very fine, and spices. Add beaten eggs and the additional pound of flour. Add almonds, which have been ground and roasted in the oven with a little sugar until light brown. Add lemon juice and rind. Mix well. Chill dough for several days before baking. Roll dough ¼" thick and cut with Christmas cookie cutters. Bake at 350° 12–15 minutes.

Ice with a thin icing. Use rosewater for flavoring. Honey Cakes keep well in a stone crock or other air-tight container.

FIG BARS

1 cup honey
1 cup shortening
1 cup sugar
2 eggs, beaten
Juice and grated rind of ½ lemon
6½ cups flour
2 teaspoons baking powder
1 teaspoon baking soda
1 teaspoon salt

Cream honey, shortening, and sugar. Add beaten eggs and lemon juice and rind. Add flour which has been sifted 3 times with baking powder, salt, and baking soda. Roll dough quite thin, cut into strips about 6" long and 3" wide. Put filling in center of the strip, and lap sides over. Bake 15 minutes at 400°. Cool. Cut crosswise into desired size.

FIG FILLING:

4 cups minced figs
1 cup honey and ¼ cup water
Juice of ½ lemon and ½ orange

Combine and cook 15 minutes, stirring constantly. Cool before using.

HERMITS

½ cup shortening
1 cup honey
½ cup brown sugar, firmly packed
2 eggs, well beaten
3 tablespoons milk
2¼ cups flour
1 teaspoon baking soda
½ teaspoon cinnamon
½ teaspoon allspice
1 cup raisins
1 cup currants
1 cup dates
½ cup nuts

Cream shortening, add honey, sugar, well-beaten eggs, milk, dry ingredients, fruit and nuts. Drop from teaspoon upon a greased cookie sheet. Bake at 400° for 10–12 minutes. Makes about 8 dozen.

ALL-HONEY COOKIES

1 cup honey
1 cup shortening
3¾ cups flour
4½ teaspoons plus a pinch baking powder
¼ teaspoon minus a pinch baking soda
½ teaspoon each cinnamon, cloves, and allspice

Heat honey and shortening together about 1 minute. Cool. Sift flour, baking powder, baking soda, and spices together. Add flour mixture to first mixture to make a soft dough.

Roll thin, cut into shapes, and bake at 350° for 12–15 minutes.

CHOCOLATE CHIP COOKIES

½ cup shortening
½ cup honey
1 small egg
1 cup sifted flour
1 teaspoon baking powder
¼ teaspoon salt
½ teaspoon vanilla extract
1½ cup semisweet chocolate chips
¼ cup chopped nuts

Cream shortening and honey until light and fluffy. Add egg and beat well.

Into another bowl sift flour, baking powder, and salt, twice. Add flour mixture to shortening mixture; add vanilla and blend all well. Fold in chocolate chips and nuts. Chill and drop by teaspoons on greased cookie sheet. Bake at 375° for 12 minutes.

PECAN BUTTERBALLS

1 cup butter
¼ cup honey
2 cups sifted flour
½ teaspoon salt
2 teaspoons vanilla extract
2 cups finely chopped pecans
Powdered sugar

Cream butter; add honey gradually; add flour, salt, and vanilla. Mix well and add chopped nuts. Form into very small balls and place on a greased baking sheet. Bake at 300° for 40–45 minutes. Remove from pan and roll in powdered sugar while still hot. Cool, roll again in the powdered sugar.

HONEY NUT BROWNIES

1/4 cup shortening
2 squares unsweetened chocolate
1/2 cup honey
1 teaspoon vanilla extract
1/2 cup sugar
2 eggs
1/2 cup flour
1/4 teaspoon baking powder
1/4 teaspoon salt
1 cup chopped nuts

Melt shortening and chocolate together. Add honey, vanilla, sugar, and beaten eggs. Sift flour, baking powder, and salt; add nuts. Add this to first mixture. Line a shallow pan with parchment paper, and bake brownies at 300° for 45 minutes.

HONEY PEANUT ROCKS

1 cup shortening
1/2 cup brown sugar, firmly packed
1/2 cup honey
2 cups flour
2 1/2 teaspoons baking powder
Pinch of baking soda
1/3 cup milk
2 cups quick-cooking oats
1 cup each of chopped raisins and
    peanuts

Cream shortening. Add brown sugar and honey gradually, and cream well. Add flour sifted with baking powder and baking soda alternately with milk. Add the oats, raisins, and peanuts. Drop from a teaspoon onto a greased cookie sheet. Bake at 300° for 15–20 minutes.

HONEY BARS

1 cup honey
3 eggs, well beaten
1 teaspoon baking powder
1 1/3 cups flour
1 cup chopped nuts
2 1/2 cups chopped dates
1 teaspoon vanilla extract

Mix honey and eggs. Add baking powder and flour sifted together, chopped nuts, dates, and vanilla. Spread dough on a long, flat pan 1/4" deep. Bake at 350° for 15–20 minutes.

Cut into 1/2" x 3" strips. Roll in powdered sugar before serving.

Note: These are fine for the holidays since they can be made ahead of time and will improve in flavor.

HONEY GINGERNUTS

1 cup honey
1 cup sugar
1 cup shortening
1 egg, beaten
2 cups flour
2 teaspoons baking powder
3 teaspoons ground ginger
1 cup chopped nuts
Additional flour

Mix honey, sugar, shortening, and egg. Sift flour, baking powder, and ginger. Combine flour mixture with honey mixture. Add nuts. Add more flour, enough to make batter right consistency. Drop by teaspoonfuls on a greased cookie sheet and bake at 350°–375°.

CHRISTMAS FRUIT NUGGETS

1 cup shortening
1½ cups honey
2 eggs
3 cups sifted cake flour
3 teaspoons baking powder
¼ teaspoon salt
½ teaspoon each cloves, cinnamon,
  and nutmeg
½ cup milk
½ cup candied pineapple
1 cup candied cherries
1 cup candied raisins
1 cup walnuts

Cream shortening. Add honey and cream together. Beat eggs and add. Sift together cake flour, baking powder, salt, cloves, cinnamon, nutmeg, and add alternately with milk. Chop pineapple, cherries, raisins, and walnuts. Mix all together well. Drop by teaspoonfuls either on greased baking pan or into tiny paper cups. Bake at 375° for about 15 minutes.

HONEY NUT COOKIES

2 egg whites
½ cup honey
½ cup sugar
¼ teaspoon salt
¼ cup water
1 tablespoon flavoring
1 cup chopped black walnuts

Beat egg whites with rotary beater until stiff. Gradually add honey, beating after each addition. Continue beating until mixture is stiff.

Combine sugar, salt, and water in small saucepan. Cook until sugar is dissolved and mixture boils, stirring constantly. Cover tightly and boil 2 minutes. Uncover and boil, without stirring, until a small amount of syrup forms a firm ball in cold water (250°). Pour syrup in fine stream over egg mixture, beating constantly. Beat until cool and thickened. Add flavoring and nuts. Drop from teaspoon onto a well-buttered, floured baking sheet. Bake at 300° for 25–30 minutes, or until delicately browned. Carefully remove from sheet with sharp edge of clean knife. Store in tightly covered jar with waxed paper between each layer. Yields about 5 dozen cookies.

CHRISTMAS COOKIES

2 cups brown sugar, firmly packed
½ cup honey
¼ cup shortening
1 egg, beaten
2½ cups flour
3 teaspoons baking powder
1 teaspoon cinnamon
2 ounce of citron, minced very fine
Juice of ½ orange
Grated rind and juice of ½ lemon
½ cup almonds, blanched and chopped

Cook sugar and honey until sugar is dissolved. Add shortening and cool. Add beaten egg. Sift together the dry ingredients and add to the syrup. Add chopped fruit, fruit juices, rind, and nuts. If necessary, add just a bit more flour to handle easily. Roll ⅛" thick and cut into fancy shapes. Bake on greased cookie sheet at 350° for 10 minutes.

LEBKUCKEN

4 eggs
½ cup sugar
⅓ cup honey
1¾ cups flour
2 teaspoons baking soda
3 teaspoons cinnamon
½ teaspoon cardamom
½ teaspoon cloves
¾ cup orange peel
½ cup citron
Grated rind of ½ lemon
¾ cup shelled almonds

ICING:

Powdered sugar
Cream

Beat whole eggs until very light, add sugar, honey, and sifted dry ingredients. Beat well. Add fruits and nuts. Bake at 350° in two 10″ x 16″ pans. Ice with blended powdered sugar and cream.

HONEY PEANUT BUTTER COOKIES

½ cup shortening
½ cup honey
½ cup brown sugar, firmly packed
1 egg
½ cup peanut butter
½ teaspoon salt
1¼ cups flour
½ teaspoon baking soda

Cream shortening, honey, and sugar together until light and fluffy. Add well-beaten egg. Add peanut butter and salt.

Stir in flour and baking soda sifted together and mix well. Form into small balls of dough. Place upon greased cookie sheet. Press with a fork. Bake at 350° for 12–15 minutes.

CHRISTMAS HONEY GINGER COOKIES

2 cups sifted flour
⅛ teaspoon baking soda
⅓ cup honey
½ teaspoon ground ginger
½ teaspoon salt
½ cup sugar
2 tablespoons water
1 egg, lightly beaten
1 teaspoon orange extract
½ cup chopped crystallized ginger
½ cup chopped blanched almonds
Colored sugar or candy for decoration

Sift flour once, measure, add baking soda and sift again.

Place honey, ground ginger, salt, sugar, water, egg, and orange extract in bowl, and beat with rotary beater until well blended. Add crystallized ginger and nuts, mixing thoroughly. Stir in flour. Chill thoroughly.

Place on lightly floured board, roll ¼″ thick, and cut into fancy Christmas shapes. Brush cookies with egg and sprinkle with colored sugar or tiny Christmas candy mixtures. Bake on ungreased baking sheet at 325° for 12–15 minutes. Cool. Store in an airtight container. Yields about 5 dozen 2½″ cookies.

HONEY OATMEAL COOKIES

½ cup shortening
1 cup honey
1 egg
1½ cups sifted flour
½ teaspoon baking soda
½ teaspoon salt
1⅔ cups rolled oats
¼ cup sour milk
½ cup chopped peanuts
1 cup raisins

Cream shortening. Add the honey and blend. Stir in the egg.

Sift together dry ingredients and add oats. Add dry ingredients alternately with milk to shortening and honey mixture. Stir in nuts and raisins. Drop by spoonfuls onto a greased pan or baking sheet. Bake at 350° for 15 minutes. Yields 3 dozen cookies.

PEANUT BUTTER BROWNIES

¼ cup shortening
2 tablespoons peanut butter
3 tablespoons cocoa
½ cup sugar
1 egg
½ cup honey
¾ cup sifted flour
½ teaspoon baking powder
¼ teaspoon salt
½ cup nuts

Cream shortening and peanut butter together. Add cocoa and sugar (sifted together) a little at a time. Cream well. Add egg and beat well. Add honey a little at a time and beat until well blended.

Add baking powder, salt, and flour sifted together. Add nuts. Mix well. Spread mixture in well-greased 8" x 8" pan. Bake at 350° for 35 minutes. Cut into 1" or 2" squares for serving.

CHOCOLATE PECAN SQUARES

⅔ cup flour
½ teaspoon baking powder
½ teaspoon salt
⅓ cup shortening
2 squares baking chocolate
½ cup sugar
2 eggs, well beaten
½ cup honey
½ cup chopped pecans
1 teaspoon vanilla extract
Pecan halves

Sift flour, baking powder, and salt together. Melt shortening and chocolate together over boiling water. Add sugar to eggs and beat well. Add honey gradually and beat thoroughly. Add shortening and chocolate mixture and beat well. Add dry ingredients, nuts, and vanilla. Spread batter in a greased 8" x 8" x 2" pan. Evenly place pecan halves on batter before baking at 350° for about 40 minutes. When done, cut into squares so that a pecan half will be in center of each square.

DATE PEANUT BUTTER DROPS

½ cup shortening
¾ cup peanut butter
½ cup sugar
½ cup honey
1 teaspoon vanilla extract
2 eggs, beaten
1 cup chopped dates
2 cups sifted flour
2½ teaspoons baking powder
½ teaspoon salt
¼ cup milk

Cream together shortening, peanut butter, and sugar. Add honey and beat. Blend in vanilla. Add beaten eggs. Add dates.

Sift together flour, baking powder, and salt, and add to creamed mixture alternately with milk. Blend well. Drop by teaspoonfuls on greased baking sheet and bake at 350° for 15 minutes. Yields 4 dozen 2″ cookies.

EGGLESS HONEY COOKIES

½ cup honey
½ cup shortening
2 cups flour
½ teaspoon cinnamon
½ teaspoon cloves
1 teaspoon baking soda

DECORATION:

Powdered sugar frosting
Cinnamon candies
Green gum drops

Heat honey and shortening carefully for a minute or two. When cool add dry ingredients that have been sifted together several times. Roll out to ¼″ thickness and cut with a doughnut cutter. Bake on greased cookie sheet for 12–15 minutes at 350°.

When cold, frost with a powdered sugar frosting. Decorate with clusters of red cinnamon candies and bits of green gum drops to form holly wreath design.

CHOCOLATE FRUIT COOKIES

½ cup honey
½ cup sugar
½ cup melted shortening
2 eggs, separated and whites beaten
3 squares baking chocolate, melted
1 teaspoon baking soda
½ cup milk
2 cups flour
1 cup raisins (or chopped dates)
1 cup chopped nuts
1 teaspoon vanilla extract

Add honey and sugar to melted shortening. Add the egg yolks and beat well. Add melted chocolate.

Add baking soda to milk and then add milk and half of the flour alternately. Mix well. Add raisins and nuts with remainder of flour. Add beaten egg whites and vanilla. Drop from teaspoon on buttered baking sheet. Bake 10–15 minutes at 350°.

HONEY JAM BARS

½ cup shortening
½ cup honey
1½ cups sifted flour
1 teaspoon baking powder
½ teaspoon salt
1 teaspoon cinnamon
¼ teaspoon nutmeg
¼ teaspoon allspice
1 egg, beaten
¾ cup jam

Cream shortening. Add honey. Blend well. Add sifted dry ingredients and mix. Add beaten egg.

Spread half of the batter into a greased pan and spread with jam. Cover jam with the remaining batter. Bake at 400° for 30–35 minutes. Cut into 1" x 4" bars. Yields 2 dozen.

HONEY PEANUT COOKIES

1 cup shortening
½ cup honey
½ cup brown sugar, firmly packed
⅓ cup milk
2 cups flour
1 teaspoon baking soda
1 teaspoon baking powder
2 cups quick-cooking oats
1 cup chopped raisins
1 cup chopped peanuts

Cream the shortening; add the honey, brown sugar, and the rest of the ingredients in the order given. Roll a teaspoonful of the dough in the hands, place on an ungreased cookie sheet, flattening a little. Bake at 325° for 15–20 minutes. Yields 4–5 dozen cookies.

DESSERTS

"If you a happy cook would be,
Use honey in your recipe."

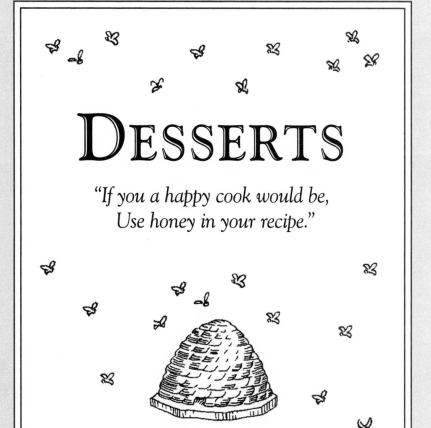

HONEYED APPLES AND CRANBERRIES

6 medium-sized apples
2¼ cups cranberries
1¾ cups water
½ cup honey
1½ cups sugar
¼ teaspoon salt
2 cinnamon sticks

Core and pare apples and place in flat-bottomed pan. Add cranberries and water and simmer 5 minutes, turning apples once during cooking period. Add remaining ingredients. Simmer 15–20 minutes longer, or until apples are tender. (Turn apples carefully during cooking so they are evenly red.)

Remove apples to dish in which they are to be served, skim the cranberry sauce and pour around apples. Cool. Cover tightly and place in refrigerator until ready to use. Yields about 8–10 portions.

HONEY-BAKED PEARS

8 pear halves
¼ cup lemon juice
½ cup honey
1 teaspoon cinnamon
2 tablespoons butter

Arrange pears in shallow buttered baking dish. Pour the lemon juice and honey over. Sprinkle with cinnamon and dot with butter. Bake at 350°. Serve hot with cream. Peaches prepared this way also make a delicious dessert.

BROILED GRAPEFRUIT

Grapefruit
Honey
Butter

Wash and dry the grapefruit and cut in half crosswise allowing one half to each person. With a sharp knife cut around and under the entire pulp being careful to leave all the membrane in the shell. Cut down on each side of each section loosening each section completely. Now with 2 fingers lift out the center core, to which will be attached the radiating membranes. This leaves the shell containing only the nicely separated fruit sections.

Spread the top of each half with honey and dot with butter. Place under the broiler flame or in a moderate oven until the honey begins to caramelize and the ingredients are well blended. Serve hot as dessert or a first course.

BAKED APPLES WITH HONEY FILLING

Apples
Honey

Wash and core the apples. Leave part of the core in the bottom of the apples to act as a plug. Fill the cavity with honey, using as much as the tartness of the apples requires. For variety, add a bit of lemon juice or a few cinnamon candies. One may stuff the cavity with raisins and dates or other fruit combinations. Bake at 350° until apples are tender.

HONEY ICE CREAM

2 cups milk
¾ cup honey
¼ teaspoon salt
2 eggs
1 cup cream

Scald 2 cups whole milk in double boiler, add honey and salt. Beat eggs in separate bowl. Pour scalded milk into the egg mixture and stir until well blended. Return to double boiler and cook for 3 or 4 minutes. Cool. Beat cream and fold into custard mixture. Freeze. Stir once or twice while freezing.

HONEY PEPPERMINT ICE CREAM FOR AN ICE CREAM FREEZER

1½ teaspoons unflavored gelatin
2 tablespoons water
½ cup milk
2½ cups light cream
⅓ cup honey
¾ cup crushed peppermint stick candy

Soak gelatin in cold water. Heat milk and cream and add honey; mix well. Add gelatin slowly, stirring constantly to prevent lumping. (Thoroughly chill if you wish to shorten freezing time.) Pour into ice cream freezer can along with crushed candy and freeze. Or if bits of the candy are desired in the ice cream, add candy after the mix has become semi-frozen. Unsweetened chocolate (1 square) cut into very small pieces may be added.

Note: A good proportion of salt and ice to use is 1 part salt to 4 parts ice.

ICE CREAM SUNDAE

Pour honey over ice cream, sprinkle nuts on top or garnish with a cherry.

MARGUERITES

Place salted crackers in a baking pan. Spread crackers with honey and chopped nuts. Place in oven until lightly browned.

HONEY APPLE CRISP

4 cups sliced apples
¼ cup sugar
1 tablespoon lemon juice
½ cup honey
½ cup flour
¼ cup brown sugar, firmly packed
¼ teaspoon salt
¼ cup butter
¼ cup walnuts (if desired)

TOPPING:
Cream
Cinnamon

Spread sliced apples in a shallow baking dish, sprinkle with sugar and lemon juice and pour honey over all.

In a bowl mix flour, brown sugar, and salt, and work in the butter as for biscuits, making a crumbly mixture. Top apples evenly with walnuts and crumb mixture. Bake at 375° for 30–40 minutes, or until apples are tender and crust crisply browned. Serve warm, with plain cream or whipped cream topped with a dash of cinnamon.

PASTRY

1½ cups flour
½ teaspoon baking powder (optional)
½ teaspoon salt
½ cup shortening
About 4 tablespoons cold water

Sift dry ingredients. Cut or work in the shortening, leaving some of the shortening in pieces the size of a pea, and add enough cold water to hold ingredients together. Toss on a floured board and roll out carefully. This makes 2 crusts.

PEACH PIE

Pastry
Peaches
1 tablespoon quick-cooking tapioca
½ cup honey

Line pie pan with pastry. Fill with sliced fresh peaches. Sprinkle with tapioca. Pour honey over peaches. Cover with strips of pastry. Bake at 425° about 40 minutes.

PECAN PIE

½ cup honey
½ cup brown sugar, firmly packed
¼ cup butter
3 eggs, beaten
1 cup broken pecans

Blend honey and sugar together. Cook slowly to form a smooth syrup. Add butter. Add beaten eggs and broken pecans. Pour into pie pan lined with pastry. Bake at 400° for 10 minutes. Reduce temperature to 350° and bake for 30 minutes, or until mixture sets.

APPLE PIE

Pastry
6 medium-sized apples (or 3 cups sliced apples)
1 tablespoon butter
1 cup honey
2 tablespoons lemon juice

Quarter and pare apples, remove core and slice. Line a 9″ pie plate with pastry. Place the sliced apples on this. Dot with bits of butter and add a perforated upper crust, pushing it toward the center. Press edges together and trim. Bake at 450° for ten minutes; then about 30 minutes at 350°, or until the crust is lightly browned and the fruit is soft. Remove from oven. Mix honey with lemon juice and carefully add through the perforations in top crust. By the time the pie is ready to serve, the honey will have been absorbed by the apples.

DEEP-DISH APPLE PIE

Pastry
Apples
1 cup honey
1 tablespoon lemon juice
Cinnamon
Butter

Wash and quarter apples. Pare. Cut into thin slices. Fill deep pie plate with apple slices. Combine honey and lemon juice; pour over apples. Sprinkle with cinnamon. Dot with butter. Cover with pastry. Prick design in crust to allow steam to escape and for decoration. Bake at 400° about 40 minutes.

BERRY PIE

Pastry
3 cups berries
¾–1 cup honey
2 tablespoons cornstarch or 4
tablespoons flour
½ teaspoon cinnamon
1 tablespoon butter

Pick over and wash berries. Place in pastry-lined pie pan. Add a little honey to cornstarch. Blend well. Add remainder of honey. Pour over berries. Add a dash of cinnamon and dot with bits of butter. Cover with crisscross pastry. Bake at 450° for 10 minutes. Reduce heat to 350° and bake 30 minutes.

PUMPKIN PIE

Pastry
2 cups stewed pumpkin
2 cups whole milk
1 cup honey
2 eggs
½ teaspoon salt
1 teaspoon cinnamon
½ teaspoon ground ginger

Mix ingredients in order given. Beat well. Pour into pastry-lined pie pan. Bake at 350° for 1 hour.

VARIATIONS:

Replace water with orange juice in pastry recipe.

For a festive note, add turkey or pumpkin designs. Roll pastry thin. Cut out using cardboard or metal pattern. Bake on cookie sheet. Place on top of baked pie.

PUMPKIN CHIFFON PIE

Baked pastry shell
1 envelope unflavored gelatin, softened
in ¼ cup cold water
1¼ cups pumpkin
½ cup honey
3 egg yolks, beaten
½ cup milk
½ teaspoon ground ginger
1 teaspoon cinnamon
½ teaspoon nutmeg
¼ teaspoon salt
3 egg whites
½ cup sugar

To the pumpkin add honey, egg yolks, milk, spices, and salt. Beat well. Cook over boiling water until mixture thickens. Add softened gelatin. Stir well. Chill until partially set. Beat egg whites with sugar and fold into pumpkin mixture. Pour into pastry shell. Chill. Serve with Honey Meringue (page 24).

HONEY CUSTARD

¼ teaspoon salt
3 eggs, lightly beaten
¼ cup honey
2 cups milk, scalded
Nutmeg

Add salt to eggs. Beat eggs just long enough to combine whites and yolks. Add honey to milk. Add honey and milk mixture slowly to eggs. Pour into custard cups. Top with a few gratings of nutmeg.

Set custard cups in pan of hot water. Bake at 325° about 40 minutes, or until custard is firm.

HONEY RAISIN PIE

1½ cups raisins
1 tablespoon grated orange rind
1 cup orange juice
¼ cup lemon juice
¾ cup honey
2 tablespoons butter
½ teaspoon salt
¼ cup cornstarch
¾ cup cold water
Pastry for double crust (9″)

Combine raisins with orange rind and juice, lemon juice, honey, butter, salt, and cornstarch that has been moistened in the cold water, and stir until blended. Bring to a boil and cook and stir until mixture thickens (about 3–4 minutes). Pour into pastry-lined pie pan, cover with top crust. Bake at 425° for 30–35 minutes. Cool before serving.

RICE RING FOR FRUIT

3 tablespoons cornstarch
½ teaspoon salt
2 eggs, separated and whites beaten
1½ cups milk
1 tablespoon butter
¼ cup honey
2 cups cooked rice

Put cornstarch and salt in top of double boiler. Add egg yolks and milk. Stir well. Cook over boiling water, stirring constantly until mixture thickens. Remove from heat. Add butter, honey, and rice. Fold in beaten whites of eggs. Turn into buttered ring mold. Bake at 350° for 30 minutes. Cool. Unmold carefully. Fill center with fruit.

CHIFFON PIE

Baked pastry shell
1 tablespoon unflavored gelatin
¼ cup cold water
3 eggs, separated
½ cup honey
¼ cup orange juice
3 tablespoons lemon juice

Soak gelatin in cold water.

Place egg yolks and honey in top of double boiler. Stir well. Add orange and lemon juices. Cook slowly over hot water, stirring constantly until thickened. Add gelatin and stir until dissolved. Remove from heat. Chill. Beat egg whites until stiff. When mixture begins to set, fold in egg whites. Pour into baked pastry shell. Chill.

HONEY DELIGHT

1 package lemon- or orange-flavored
  gelatin
½ cup boiling water
½ cup honey
Juice of ½ lemon
1 can evaporated milk, chilled
½ pound vanilla wafers, crushed

Dissolve gelatin in boiling water. Add honey and lemon juice and mix well. Whip evaporated milk and fold in. Line pan with crushed vanilla wafers, reserving some for topping. Pour mixture into pan. Place remaining crushed vanilla wafers on top of mixture and put in refrigerator to set. Cut into squares. Serves 6.

AMERICAN PUDDING

¾ cup sifted flour
1 teaspoon baking powder
½ teaspoon salt
4 tablespoons butter
⅓ cup sugar
½ cup milk
¼ cup currants
1½ teaspoons grated lemon rind
½ cup honey
1¼ cups boiling water

Sift flour once, measure, add baking powder and salt, and sift again.

Cream 2 tablespoons of the butter, add sugar gradually, creaming after each addition. Add 2 tablespoons of the milk and beat thoroughly. Add flour, alternately with remaining milk, a small amount at a time, beating after each addition until smooth. Add currants and lemon rind. Turn into well-greased 8″ x 8″ x 2″ baking dish. Combine remaining butter, honey, water, and dash of salt. Pour over batter. Bake at 350° for 40–45 minutes. Serve warm with cream. Yields about 6 portions.

PUDDING SAUCE

¼ cup sugar
6 tablespoons flour
½ cup honey
2 cups water
⅓ cup butter
Juice of 1 lemon
Juice of 1 orange

Mix sugar and flour, add honey and water. Cook in double boiler until thickened. Add butter and fruit juice. Serve hot.

CRANBERRY PUDDING

2 cups large cranberries, cut in half
    and mixed with 1½ cups flour
⅔ cup honey
⅓ cup hot water
1 teaspoon baking soda
½ teaspoon salt
½ teaspoon baking powder

Add dry ingredients to the cranberries mixed with the flour. Mix honey and hot water and add. Put in steamer and steam 2 hours. Serve with Honey Sauce (page 61).

HONEY STEAMED PUDDING

¼ cup butter
½ cup honey
1 egg, well beaten
2¼ cups sifted flour
3½ teaspoons baking powder
¼ teaspoon salt
1 cup milk
½ teaspoon vanilla extract

Sift together dry ingredients.

Cream butter, add honey gradually and then the well-beaten egg. Add the sifted dry ingredients and milk alternately. Add vanilla.

Fill buttered individual molds ¾ full. Cover loosely with wax paper held in place with a rubber band. Place molds in a steamer for 30 minutes. Test with a toothpick. Serve hot. Makes 12 molds.

HONEY HARD SAUCE

⅓ cup butter
¾ cup honey
1 teaspoon lemon juice

Cream the butter and gradually beat in honey. Add lemon juice. Chill.

HONEY SAUCE

½ cup butter
⅔ cup honey
2 tablespoons flour
2 eggs, lightly beaten
½ cup lemon juice
½ pint whipping cream, whipped

Mix and cook first 4 ingredients slowly in double boiler until thickened. Remove from heat. Add lemon juice. When cool and ready to serve, fold in whipped cream.

RICE PUDDING

2 cups cooked rice
3 cups milk
¾ cup honey
3 eggs
1 cup chopped raisins
Cream (optional)

Mix rice, milk and honey. Add the eggs which have been lightly beaten. Stir in the chopped raisins. Bake at about 350° in a well-greased baking dish for about 1 hour. Serve with cream if desired. Serves 8.

FRENCH APPLE DUMPLING

2 cups flour
4 teaspoons baking powder
½ teaspoon salt
¼ cup shortening
¾ cup milk
4 large apples, sliced
½ cup sugar
¼ teaspoon cinnamon
Melted butter

HONEY DUMPLING SAUCE:

1½ cups honey
2 tablespoons cornstarch
1½ cups water
⅛ teaspoon salt
1 tablespoon butter
½ teaspoon vanilla extract

Mix ingredients as for biscuit dough. Handle as lightly as possible. On a floured towel, roll out the dough ¼" thick. Cover the dough with the sliced apples and sprinkle them with the sugar and cinnamon. Roll up like a jelly roll and cut into 1" slices. (Makes 8 slices.) Place slices in a buttered baking pan. Put 1 teaspoon melted butter over each roll. Bake at 400° 20–25 minutes.

To prepare Honey Dumpling Sauce, mix all ingredients except vanilla; cook until clear. Add vanilla. Serve on the hot slices.

TART PASTRY

2 cups flour
½ teaspoon salt
½ cup shortening
1 cup cottage cheese
3 tablespoons honey

Sift dry ingredients and cut in shortening as for pie pastry. Add honey to the cheese. Add cheese to the flour mixture and blend with pastry cutter or knives. If cheese is not moist enough to make a good pastry, add a few drops of cold water. Roll thin on lightly floured board.

RHUBARB TARTS

2 cups rhubarb cut in ½" pieces
2 eggs yolks
¾ cup honey
3 tablespoons flour
¼ teaspoon salt
2 tablespoons honey
Tart pastry

MERINGUE:

2 tablespoons honey
2 egg whites

Wash rhubarb and cut into ½" lengths. Pour boiling water over the rhubarb and drain in colander.

Mix lightly beaten egg yolks with honey, flour, and salt. Add to rhubarb. Pour into pastry-lined muffin pans. Bake at 350° for 30 minutes or until done.

Top with meringue made by adding honey to stiffly beaten egg whites.

BANBURY TARTS

1 cup chopped raisins
¾ cup honey
3 tablespoons cracker crumbs
1 lightly beaten egg
1 tablespoon melted butter
⅛ teaspoon salt
½ lemon, juice and grated rind
Tart pastry

Combine all ingredients except pastry. Roll Tart Pastry thin and cut into 3" squares. Place a teaspoon of raisin mixture in the center of each square; fold into a triangle and press edges together. Prick several times to allow steam to escape. Bake at 450° for 15 minutes.

COVENTRY TARTLETS

Tart pastry
Red or green honey jelly

FILLING:

½ pound cottage or cream cheese
½ cup honey
¼ cup butter
2 egg yolks
½ teaspoon salt
¼ teaspoon nutmeg
1 tablespoon orange juice

Mix filling ingredients until creamy.

Roll Tart Pastry thin; line a dozen individual tart molds. Prick and fill with cheese mixture. Bake at 450° for 10 minutes, reduce the heat to 325° and bake until golden brown and firm. Remove from the oven and cool.

When ready to serve, garnish with red or green honey jelly.

HONEY PARFAIT

2 eggs, separated
Pinch salt
½ cup honey
1 teaspoon vanilla extract
1⅔ cups evaporated milk, chilled

Beat egg whites until foamy. Gradually add honey while beating constantly. Add egg yolks and vanilla. Beat until well blended. Fold in stiffly beaten, chilled milk. Garnish with maraschino cherries. Pour into freezing trays. Serves 8.

RHUBARB MEDLEY

3 cups rhubarb
1 cup honey
Cinnamon candies
2 eggs, separated and whites beaten
1 tablespoon unflavored gelatin
Whipped cream

Wash rhubarb and cut into pieces of about 1″ in length. Place in saucepan. Add honey and enough water to prevent it from scorching. Cover and cook slowly until tender. During last five minutes, add enough cinnamon candies to give it a deep pink color.

Add a little of the hot mixture to egg yolks. Return to saucepan.

Soften 1 tablespoon of gelatin in a little cold water in large bowl. Gradually add hot mixture to this. Just before it begins to set, fold in the 2 stiffly beaten egg whites. Pour into molds and chill. Serve with whipped cream.

TAPIOCA CREAM

⅓ cup quick-cooking tapioca
⅓ cup honey
¼ teaspoon salt
2 eggs, separated and whites beaten
4 cups milk, scalded
1 teaspoon vanilla extract
Cream

Combine tapioca, honey, salt, and egg yolks in top of double boiler. Add milk slowly and mix thoroughly. Cook until tapioca is transparent, stirring often. Remove from the heat and fold into the stiffly beaten egg whites. Add the vanilla. This may be served either warm or cold with cream.

RHUBARB BROWN BETTY

2 cups bread crumbs
3 cups rhubarb cut in ½″ pieces
  (apples may be substituted)
½ cup honey
¼ cup water
½ teaspoon nutmeg
3 tablespoons butter

Mix ¾ of the bread crumbs and ¾ fruit and place in a deep baking dish. Bring honey and water to a boil. Pour over bread and fruit mixture. Sprinkle remainder of crumbs over this, sprinkle with nutmeg, and dot with butter. Arrange the rest of the fruit so that each serving will have one or more pieces of fruit on top. Bake at 325° for 30–40 minutes.

MEATS

"A drop or two of Nature's sweet
Will give a better taste to meat."

BAKED HAM

1 ham
1 cup honey
Whole cloves

Select a good quality ham. Wipe meat with a damp cloth and remove unsightly parts. Place ham fat side up in roasting pan. Add no water. Bake uncovered at 300°. Insert a meat thermometer with the bulb at the center of the largest muscle. Cook until the thermometer registers an internal temperature of 170° (about 25–30 minutes per pound should be allowed for roasting time). Before the ham is done, take from the oven and remove the rind. Mark fat into squares. Place whole clove in each square. Glaze ham with honey or see Honey Glazes. Return to oven to finish baking. Baste frequently.

DECORATIVE VARIATION:

Fix orange slices and maraschino cherries in place on ham with cloves.

HONEY-SPICED BROILED HAM

1 slice ham, 1" thick
¾ cup honey
½ teaspoon cloves
½ teaspoon allspice
½ teaspoon cinnamon

Wipe meat with a damp cloth. Place meat on a broiler rack allowing 3 inches between the top of the meat and source of heat, if possible. Sprinkle with half the spices and cook until browned, basting with the honey occasionally. When brown, turn over. Sprinkle other side with remaining spices and continue cooking, basting occasionally with remaining honey.

HONEY GLAZES

Mix chopped maraschino cherries, whole almonds, and 1 cup honey.

Mix 1 cup honey with 1 cup apricot pulp. (For decoration, use apricot halves in flower design with whole cloves or angelica as stems.)

Mix crushed pineapple with 1 cup honey.

Mix tart cherries with honey.

Mix 1 cup honey with ½ cup orange juice.

Mix 1 cup honey with ½ cup cranberry sauce.

Mix 1 cup honey with ½ cup cider.

FRUITED AND HONEYED CANADIAN BACON

6 slices Canadian bacon
1 cup water
1 cup honey
1 cup raisins
6 slices pineapple

Have bacon sliced ½" thick. Place in dripping pan and into oven at 350°. Bring water to the boiling point, add the honey, stir until well mixed; then add raisins and simmer for 10 minutes. When the meat has been in the oven for 1 hour, place a slice of pineapple over each piece of bacon, pour the honey syrup containing the raisins over the bacon and pineapple. Return to the oven for 15 minutes.

LAMB CHOPS WITH HONEY MINT SAUCE

Select rib, loin, or shoulder lamb chops. Place the chops in the oven so that there is a distance of about 3 inches between the top of the chops and the broiler. If the distance must be less, reduce the temperature accordingly so that the chops will broil at a moderate temperature. When the chops are browned on one side, season, turn and finish the cooking on the second side. Frequently during broiling, baste with Honey Mint Sauce below. Chops cut 1" thick require 12–15 minutes for broiling.

HONEY MINT SAUCE

½ cup water
1 tablespoon vinegar
1 cup honey
¼ cup chopped mint

Heat the water and the vinegar. Add the honey, stir well, then add the chopped mint. Cook slowly for five minutes. This sauce can be used to baste lamb chops or lamb roast during cooking or can be served with the meat at the table.

RAISIN SAUCE

1 cup raisins
1 cup water
¼ cup honey
1 tablespoon lemon juice

Put raisins and water in saucepan. Simmer until raisins are plumped. Add honey. Boil gently for fifteen minutes. Just before serving, add lemon juice.

SWEET HORSERADISH SAUCE

¼ cup honey
¼ cup mayonnaise
½ cup whipping cream
3 tablespoons horseradish
1 teaspoon mustard
¼ teaspoon salt
1 teaspoon vinegar

Add honey to mayonnaise. Whip cream and fold in. Add horseradish, mustard, salt, and vinegar. Store in refrigerator until ready to use.

SALADS

*"If honey is used with the fruit
The flavor will your palate suit."*

FRENCH SALAD BOWL

Bread loaf
Garlic
Crisp salad greens

Place a crust of bread rubbed with garlic in large bowl while tossing the salad with Honey French Dressing (page 72). Use any one or a combination of crisp salad greens such as lettuce, romaine, watercress, endive, pepper grass, or chicory. Serve at once.

PEAR SALAD

Pears
Pimento cheese
Honey French Dressing (page 72)
Lettuce

If canned pears are used, place can in refrigerator to chill pears before making up salad. Allow one half pear per person. Place cut side down on lettuce. Cover pear with riced pimento cheese and serve with Honey French Dressing. (Rice cheese the same way one rices potatoes.)

COLE SLAW

1 cup chilled sour cream
¼ cup vinegar
¼ cup honey
1 teaspoon salt
2 teaspoons celery salt
4 cups finely shredded cabbage

Beat sour cream until thick; add vinegar, honey, salt, and celery salt. Mix into shredded cabbage.

AVOCADO SALAD

Avocado
Grapefruit
Lettuce
Honey
Lemon juice
Berries
Paprika or chopped parsley (optional)

Combine equal parts of honey and lemon juice. Beat well and serve over slices of avocado and sections of grapefruit on crisp lettuce. Garnish with berries.

NOTE: A dash of paprika or chopped parsley may be added if desired.

STUFFED TOMATO SALAD

Select even-sized, firm red tomatoes. Wash, scald in boiling water to loosen skin. Remove skin. Hollow the tomatoes. Sprinkle inside with salt. Drain. Chill. Fill and pile high with (1) chicken, tuna, ham, or seafood salad; (2) cole slaw; or (3) cottage cheese and chives. Top with a spoonful of honeyed mayonnaise and stuffed olive.

LEMON-CREAM SALAD DRESSING

3 tablespoons honey
1 tablespoon lemon juice
1 cup whipped cream

Combine honey and lemon juice. Add to whipped cream. Serve on fruit salad.

BOILED DRESSING

1 teaspoon dry mustard
1 teaspoon salt
1/8 teaspoon cayenne pepper
2 tablespoons flour
1 cup milk
3 tablespoons honey
2 egg yolks
1/2 cup vinegar
1 tablespoon butter

Mix dry ingredients in top of double boiler, add milk, honey, and egg yolks. Stir well. Cook over hot water until thickened. Add vinegar and butter. Mix well until smooth mixture is formed.

THOUSAND ISLAND DRESSING

Finely mince a few stuffed olives, a small onion, and a little green pepper. Combine with 1 cup mayonnaise and 1/2 cup chili sauce. Fold in 1/2 cup whipped cream.

HONEY FRENCH DRESSING

1/2 cup honey
1 cup salad oil
1/2 teaspoon salt
1/3 cup chili sauce
1/2 cup vinegar
1 medium onion, grated
1 tablespoon Worcestershire sauce

Place all ingredients in a jar and shake well.

Note: Place a portion of Frozen Fruit Salad (page 73) on top of lettuce leaf and top with this dressing.

FRENCH DRESSING

1/2 cup salad oil
1/2 cup lemon juice
1/2 cup honey
1/2 teaspoon paprika
1/2 teaspoon salt

Place all in a tightly covered jar and shake vigorously just before using.

ROQUEFORT CHEESE DRESSING

Crumble 1/4 pound Roquefort cheese into small pieces. Add to 1 cup French Dressing (above).

FRUIT SALAD

White seedless grapes
1 orange
1 banana
1 pear or peach
1 small apple
1 lemon
Lettuce
Honey

Cut grapes into halves. Cut orange into halves and remove sections with a sharp-pointed knife. Slice banana and pear or peach and dice the apple. Pour lemon juice over apple and banana. Moisten all fruit with honey and serve on crisp lettuce or chicory.

FROZEN FRUIT SALAD

4 ounces cream cheese
3 tablespoons mayonnaise
2 tablespoons honey
1 cup pitted white cherries
3 slices pineapple, cut into small pieces
½ pint whipping cream

Combine cream cheese with mayonnaise, add honey, and mix well. Add cherries and pineapple. Whip cream and fold in. Place in freezing tray.

Place a portion of Frozen Fruit Salad on top of lettuce leaf and top with Honey French Dressing (page 72).

FRUIT SALAD PLATTER

Place a small dish filled with salad dressing in center of a large platter. Place a large cuplike lettuce leaf for each person around the bowl. In each lettuce leaf place canned pear half, fig, peach, cherries, or other fruit.

Prunes stuffed with equal parts peanut butter and honey, or cream cheese and honey, may be placed between salads for garnish; or small cheese balls made by adding enough honey to cream cheese to soften, then make into ball shape, and roll in finely chopped nuts or finely chopped parsley.

FRUIT SALAD DRESSING

½ cup lemon juice or other fruit juice
2 teaspoons flour
⅛ teaspoon salt
¼ cup honey
2 eggs yolks
1 cup whipped cream

Blend lemon juice, flour, salt, and honey until smooth. Cook in the top of double boiler until thickened. Beat yolks of eggs and gradually add the lemon mixture. When well blended return to double boiler and cook about 2 minutes until custardlike in texture. Remove from heat and chill. When ready to use, fold in 1 cup of whipped cream.

DRESSING FOR FRUIT

1 egg
1 tablespoon cornstarch
Pinch of salt
2 tablespoons honey
1 cup pineapple juice
2 tablespoons lemon juice

Put lightly beaten egg, cornstarch, salt, and honey in top of double boiler. Add juices. Cook slowly over hot water until mixture thickens.

SANDWICHES

"Let honey add that flavor rare
To sandwiches that you prepare."

HONEY BUTTER

½ cup butter
½ to 1 cup honey

Cream butter well. Add honey gradually. Beat thoroughly. Place in refrigerator. Delicious on toast, hot breads, waffles, and for sandwich filling.

TEA SANDWICHES

With a biscuit cutter cut circles from bread slices. Spread with softened butter and top with cream cheese softened with honey. On this, spread red raspberry jam. Place a dot of cream cheese mixture or whipped cream in the center.

TOASTED TEA SANDWICHES

Use circles cut from bread as in above recipe. Toast on both sides. Spread with Honey Butter (above). Sprinkle with chopped nuts. Place under broiler until nuts are lightly browned and serve while hot.

ROLLED SANDWICHES

Spread creamed Honey Butter (left) on thinly sliced, crustless bread. Sprinkle with chopped nuts. Roll, slice, and fasten with toothpick. Seal open edge with honey butter. Cover with waxed paper. Chill.

CREAM CHEESE SANDWICH FILLING

Soften cream cheese with enough honey to spread well. Add chopped raisins or nuts.

FRUIT FILLING

¼ cup each dried prunes, dates, figs,
   and orange peel
1 tablespoon candied ginger
¼ cup honey

Chop fruit and candied ginger. Blend with honey. Use between slices of buttered bread.

VEGETABLES

*"Here honey lends refining touch
If not too spare or not too much."*

BAKED BEANS

Soak 2 cups washed beans in 4 cups of cold water over night. Drain off any water that has not been absorbed.

Cover the beans with fresh cold water and cook on low in a tightly covered saucepan. Do not allow the beans to boil. Let them simmer for 1¼ hours. Again drain the beans, saving the water.

Prepare the bean pot by placing about ½ pound of scored salt pork in the bottom. Add the beans.

Add ½ cup of honey to the water that has been drained from the beans (or plain boiling water if no bean water was left over). Pour over beans in pot.

In a bowl, mix 1 teaspoon salt, 1 teaspoon dry mustard, 1 teaspoon ginger, if desired, and 1 tablespoon of finely chopped onion with a little of the honey water. Add remainder of the honey bean water to this seasoning and pour over the beans. Place small pieces of salt pork on top (bacon may be used). Cover bean pot and bake in a low oven about 6 hours. Uncover the bean pot during the last hour of baking. If the beans become too dry, it may be necessary to add a little water.

HONEY-BAKED SQUASH

Wash squash and cut in half lengthwise. Remove seeds. To each half add 1 tablespoon of honey and 1 or 2 little pork sausage links. Bake at 400° until squash is tender and sausages brown.

SWEET-SOUR CABBAGE

4 cups shredded cabbage
½ cup diced bacon
3 tablespoons flour
¼ cup honey
¼ cup vinegar
½ cup water
1 teaspoon onion, chopped

Cook shredded cabbage in boiling salted water until tender. Drain. Cook bacon until crisp and remove from pan; place on cabbage. Blend bacon fat with flour. Add honey, vinegar, water, and chopped onion. Cook until thickened. Pour over cabbage and bacon. Season to taste. Serve hot.

Note: This same recipe may be used with cooked potatoes instead of cabbage.

GLAZED ONIONS OR CARROTS

Cook small white onions or carrots in boiling salted water about 20–30 minutes, or until tender. Drain. Let stand a few minutes to dry. Melt 4 tablespoons butter in pan. Add ¼ cup honey. When well blended, add onions or carrots and cook slowly until browned and well glazed. Turn vegetables occasionally for an even glaze.

FAMILY BEETS

Beets
1 tablespoon cornstarch
½ cup vinegar
Few whole cloves
¾ cup honey
1 tablespoon butter

Cook beets, slice, and keep warm.

To prepare the sauce, combine honey, cornstarch, vinegar, and a few whole cloves. Bring to a slow boil and boil 5 minutes. Add butter. Pour over beets and let stand 20 minutes. Serve hot.

SCALLOPED TOMATOES

2 cups cooked tomatoes
½ teaspoon salt
Pepper
2 tablespoons butter
2 tablespoons honey
1 cup cracker crumbs

Cover bottom of buttered baking dish with a layer of tomatoes. On this sprinkle salt, pepper, dots of butter, and honey. Cover with a layer of cracker crumbs. Repeat with another layer of tomatoes, crumbs, and seasoning. Bake 20 minutes in a hot oven.

CANDIED SWEET POTATOES

Boil 6 medium-sized sweet potatoes without paring them. When tender, drain and remove the skins. Cut in half lengthwise and arrange in a buttered baking dish. Season with salt. Heat ¼ cup butter, ½ cup honey, and ½ cup orange juice, add to potatoes. Bake at 400° until potatoes are brown.

SWEET POTATO-ORANGE CASSEROLE

6 cooked and sliced sweet potatoes
¼ cup butter
2 small oranges
½ cup honey
½ cup orange juice
¼ cup buttered bread crumbs

Place a layer of sliced sweet potatoes in a greased baking dish. Dot with butter and place a layer of sliced orange (not peeled) on top. Repeat this arrangement of sweet potatoes and orange slices. Mix honey with orange juice and pour over all. Cover with buttered bread crumbs. Cover and bake about 30 minutes at 375°. Remove cover last 10 minutes to brown crumbs.

Book Two

THE HONEY RECIPE BOOK

BREADS AND PASTRIES

HONEY APPLESAUCE-OATMEAL BREAD

½ cup honey
1 tablespoon honey
½ cup shortening
1 cup applesauce
⅜ cup lukewarm milk
2 packets active dry yeast
2 eggs
3 cups sifted flour
1 cup rolled oats
1½ teaspoons salt
⅓ cup chopped nuts
Cinnamon
Nutmeg

APPLESAUCE TOPPING:

1 cup applesauce
2 tablespoons butter
¼ cup honey
½ cup flaked coconut

Combine honey, shortening, and applesauce. Heat until shortening melts. Cool to lukewarm.

Combine milk, 1 tablespoon honey, and yeast, stirring until yeast dissolves. Let stand 5–10 minutes.

Beat eggs in large bowl. Add lukewarm applesauce mixture, yeast mixture, and flour. Mix to smooth batter. Add oats and salt, mix well. Cover and let rise until double in bulk.

Beat batter again, spread batter in a greased 8″ round springform pan.

Prepare Applesauce Topping by slowly cooking applesauce down to ½ cup and combining with butter, honey, and coconut.

Spread topping on dough. Sprinkle with nuts, cinnamon, and nutmeg. Cover and let rise until double in bulk. Bake at 375° for 50–60 minutes or until done.

APPLE-ORANGE HONEY LOAF

2 large oranges
1 cup raisins
2 cups applesauce
1 cup honey
4 cups sifted flour
4 teaspoons baking powder
1½ teaspoons baking soda
1 cup sugar
1½ teaspoons salt
1½ cups chopped nuts
2 eggs, beaten
6 tablespoons melted butter or
  margarine

Squeeze juice from oranges. Using medium blade, put rind and raisins through food processor. Add orange juice, rind, and raisins to applesauce; stir in honey.

Sift together flour, baking powder, baking soda, sugar, and salt into a large bowl. Add applesauce mixture and nuts; mix thoroughly; add eggs and melted butter or margarine; stir until thoroughly blended. Pour into 2 greased 9″ x 5″ x 3″ loaf pans. Bake at 350° 1 hour and 15 minutes. Remove from pans and cool on wire rack. The bread will slice better if allowed to stand 12 hours.

HONEY-FILLED COFFEE CAKE

2 cakes compressed or 2 packets dry
    granular yeast
1/4 cup lukewarm water
1/2 cup shortening
2 teaspoons salt
1/4 cup sugar
1 cup scalded milk
2 eggs, beaten
4 1/2 cups sifted flour

HONEY FILLING:

1/2 cup honey
1/4 cup sugar
Grated rind of 1 orange or lemon
1 tablespoon orange or lemon juice
1 teaspoon cinnamon
1/3 cup raisins, cut fine
1/3 cup nuts, chopped fine
1 tablespoon melted butter or
    margarine

HONEY GLAZE:

1/2 cup honey
1/2 cup sugar
1 tablespoon butter or margarine
1 tablespoon coarsely grated orange
    rind.

Sprinkle granular yeast over warm (110°) water or crumble compressed yeast over lukewarm (85°) water. Let stand until thoroughly dissolved, about 5–15 minutes.

Combine shortening, salt, and sugar in large bowl; add scalded milk. Stir until shortening is melted, then cool until lukewarm. Add eggs and yeast; mix well. Add flour gradually, beating thoroughly after each addition.

Turn onto lightly floured board and knead to a smooth dough. Place in greased bowl and brush top of dough with melted shortening. Cover; let rise in warm place until light and doubled, (about 1½ hours). Punch down and let rest 10 minutes. Turn out onto floured board. Divide dough in half, keeping one half covered with cloth.

Roll out the other half into a rectangle, about 12" x 16". Brush with melted butter. Make Honey Filling by combining all its ingredients together and spread half the filling over the rectangle. Roll like jelly roll; seal edges. Cut into 1" slices.

Make bottom layer in 10" greased tube pan by placing slices (cut side down) so they barely touch. Arrange remaining slices in layers, covering up the spaces—with no slice directly on top of another. (This gives an interesting swirl pattern when coffee cake is sliced.)

Prepare remaining half of dough in same manner, placing slices on top in layers as before. Cover and let rise in warm place about 30 minutes or until doubled. Bake at 350° for 45–60 minutes, or until sides and top are well browned. (If bread browns too soon, cover with foil the last half of baking.) Loosen cake from pan; turn out on rack to cool.

Make Honey Glaze by combining all its ingredients together and simmer until thickened, about 5 minutes. Drizzle over cake.

HONEY PECAN WHEAT ROLLS

1 cup milk
3 tablespoons molasses
2 tablespoons honey
2½ teaspoons salt
4 tablespoons shortening
½ cup warm, not hot, water
   (lukewarm for compressed yeast)
1 cake compressed or 1 packet dry
   granular yeast
2¼ cups whole wheat flour
2¼ cups white flour
1 cup chopped pecans

HONEY SYRUP:

⅓ cup brown sugar, firmly packed
⅔ cup honey
3 tablespoons butter

Scald milk. Stir in molasses, honey, salt, and shortening; cool to lukewarm. Measure water into a large mixing bowl. Sprinkle or crumble in yeast. Stir until dissolved. Stir in lukewarm milk mixture. Mix flours; add about half to the liquid. Beat until smooth. Add remaining flour. Turn out on lightly floured board. Knead until smooth and elastic. Place in a greased bowl. Brush top with shortening. Cover; let rise in a warm place, free from draft, about 1 hour and 20 minutes, until doubled in bulk. Punch down. Turn out on lightly floured board.

Combine and stir ingredients for Honey Syrup. Spread half of the syrup in each of two 8" x 8" x 2" pans. Arrange half the pecans in each pan.

Divide dough in half. Form each half into a 1" roll. Cut into 12 equal pieces.

Form into balls. Place in prepared pans about ¼" apart. Cover; let rise in a warm place, free from draft, about 1 hour, until doubled in bulk.

Bake at 400° about 25 minutes. Turn out of pans immediately. Makes 2 dozen.

HONEY BUNS

¼ cup warm water
1 teaspoon sugar
1 cake compressed or 1 packet dry
   granular yeast
½ cup shortening
½ cup sugar
1 teaspoon salt
3 cups sifted flour
¾ cup water
1 egg, well beaten
½ cup honey
½ cup chopped nuts

Combine warm water and 1 teaspoon sugar. Sprinkle granular yeast over warm (110°) mixture; or crumble compressed yeast over lukewarm (85°) mixture. Let stand 5 minutes.

Cream shortening, ½ cup sugar, and salt. Mix in 1 cup flour and ¾ cup water. Add to yeast mixture and stir in 2 cups flour and egg.

Cover and refrigerate overnight.

Grease muffin pans, enough for 24 buns. In each muffin cup put 1 teaspoon each honey and nuts. Drop 1 tablespoon of dough in each muffin cup. Let rise in warm place until doubled. Bake at 375° for 12–15 minutes. Serve upside down.

BASIC SWEET DOUGH FOR HONEY ROSEBUDS

½ cup milk
½ cup sugar
¼ cup shortening
1½ teaspoons salt
½ cup warm, not hot, water
2 cakes compressed or 2 packets dry granular yeast
2 eggs, beaten
5 cups sifted flour

Scald milk; stir in sugar, shortening, and salt. Cool to lukewarm.

Measure water into a large mixing bowl (warm, not hot, for dry yeast; lukewarm for compressed yeast). Sprinkle or crumble in yeast; stir until dissolved. Blend in lukewarm milk mixture. Add egg and about half the flour. Beat until smooth.

Stir in remaining flour to form a soft dough. Turn out on a floured board. Knead until smooth and elastic. Place in greased bowl. Brush with softened shortening. Cover; let rise in warm place, free from draft, about 1 hour until doubled in bulk. Punch down.

Note: Dough may be used with many toppings. See below for one such recipe.

HONEY ROSEBUD TOPPING:

¼ cup honey
⅓ cup chopped nuts
½ cup dried currants or chopped raisins

Divide Sweet Dough in half. Roll each half into a square about 12″ x 12″. Brush each square with honey. Sprinkle with currants and chopped nuts.

Roll as for jelly roll. Cut into 12 equal pieces. Place cut side up in greased muffin pans. With sharp knife or scissors, cut crosses about ½″ deep across top of buns. Cover. Let rise in a warm place, free from draft, until doubled in bulk. Bake at 350° about 30 minutes.

QUICK APPLESAUCE PINWHEELS

2 cups applesauce
2 tablespoons butter or margarine
⅓ cup honey
⅔ cup raisins
1 package roll mix
2 tablespoons sugar
Cinnamon

Combine applesauce, butter or margarine, and honey; cook 15–20 minutes to evaporate some of the moisture and thicken. Add raisins and cool.

Prepare roll mix according to directions on package, adding sugar to roll mix. After dough has risen double in bulk, knead. Roll out in oblong 15″ x 11″ x ½″. Spread with applesauce mixture. Sprinkle generously with cinnamon. Roll up like jelly roll. Cut in 1″ slices. Place slices close together in greased 9″ x 9″ x 2″ pan, cut side up. Cover; let rise until doubled. Bake at 400° for 25 minutes. Serve hot.

In early England, France, and Germany, honey was diluted with fruit juices and fermented to make mead, an ale which made men "strong and brawny."

HONEY BUN COFFEE CAKE

1 cake compressed or 1 packet dry
   granular yeast
¼ cup water (lukewarm for
   compressed yeast, warm for dry)
½ cup milk
¼ cup sugar
1 teaspoon salt
2 tablespoons shortening
1 egg
1 teaspoon grated lemon rind (if
   desired)
3 cups sifted flour
¼ cup butter or margarine
2 tablespoons honey
1 egg white
1 cup confectioners sugar

Soften yeast in water. Scald milk; cool to lukewarm. Measure sugar, salt, and shortening into medium-size mixing bowl. Add flour (about 1 cup) to make a thick batter. Mix well. Add softened yeast, egg, and lemon rind. Beat well. Add enough more flour (about 1½ cups) to make a soft dough.

Turn out on lightly floured board or pastry cloth and knead until smooth and satiny. Place in greased bowl. Cover and let rise until doubled (about 1½ hours). When light, punch down and let rest 10 minutes.

Divide dough into 12 equal pieces. Roll each piece under palm of hands to roll about 8" long and ¾" in diameter. Make 6 of the rolls into "U" shaped pieces and arrange side by side in bottom of greased 9" round pan with ends toward center forming a scalloped circle. Make remaining 6 rolls into oval shaped pieces.

Arrange pieces in pan so that ends meet in the center and each oval covers joining ends of 2 "U" shaped pieces. Cream together butter or margarine and honey. Add unbeaten egg white. Mix well. Add sugar and blend thoroughly. Pour over coffee cake in pan. Let rise until doubled (about 45 minutes). Bake at 350° about 25 minutes.

HONEY MARMALADE-NUT BREAD

2½ cups sifted flour
1 tablespoon baking powder
1 teaspoon salt
½ cup honey
2 tablespoons soft butter or margarine
3 eggs, beaten
1 cup orange marmalade
1 tablespoon grated orange peel
1 cup finely chopped walnuts or pecans

Sift flour with baking powder and salt; set aside.

In medium bowl, with wooden spoon, beat honey, butter, and eggs until smooth. Stir in marmalade and orange peel, mixing well. Add flour mixture, stirring until well combined. Stir in nuts. Pour into greased and floured loaf pan. Bake at 350° about 1 hour or until cake tester inserted in center comes out clean. Let cool in pan 10 minutes. Remove from pan; cool completely on wire rack. Cut into thin slices, and serve with butter or cream cheese.

BROWN NUT BREAD WITH HONEY GLAZE

3 cups whole wheat flour
2 cups buttermilk
½ cup honey
2 tablespoons sugar
3 teaspoons baking soda
1 teaspoon salt
¼ teaspoon nutmeg
1 cup chopped pecans

HONEY GLAZE:

1 tablespoon honey
1 tablespoon melted butter

Mix dry ingredients well. Blend honey with milk and mix into dry ingredients. Grease one 9" x 5" x 3" loaf pan and pour in mixture. Bake in 350° oven for 45 minutes or until done.

Remove from oven. Glaze top with honey and butter mixture. Sprinkle with chopped pecans. Return to oven for 5 more minutes.

HONEY WHOLE WHEAT MUFFINS

1 cup sifted flour
2 teaspoons baking powder
½ teaspoon salt
½ cup unsifted whole wheat flour
½ cup milk
1 egg, well beaten
½ cup honey
½ cup coarsely chopped cooked prunes
1 teaspoon grated orange peel
¼ cup salad oil or melted shortening

Grease bottoms of twelve 2½" muffin-pan cups, or line with muffin papers.

Sift flour with baking powder and salt into large bowl. Stir in whole wheat flour; mix well.

Combine milk and rest of ingredients in medium bowl; beat well with wooden spoon. Make a well in center of dry ingredients. Pour in milk mixture all at once; stir quickly with fork, just until dry ingredients are moistened. Do not beat. Batter will be lumpy. Quickly spoon batter into muffin-pan cups, filling not quite ⅔ full. Bake at 400° for 20–25 minutes or until nicely browned. Loosen edge of each muffin with spatula; turn out. Serve hot.

QUICK HONEY ORANGE ROLLS

1 tablespoon orange juice
2 teaspoons grated orange rind
½ cup strained honey
¼ cup butter
2 cups prepared biscuit mix (or 1 biscuit recipe using 2 cups flour)
¾ cup milk

Make a thin syrup with the orange juice, grated rind, honey, and butter. Pour equal amounts into eight greased custard cups.

Blend the biscuit mix with the milk and drop an equal amount of the dough into each cup. Bake at 450° for 12–15 minutes.

QUICK HONEY COCONUT BUNS

3 cups sifted flour
3¾ teaspoons baking powder
1 teaspoon salt
⅓ cup granulated sugar
½ cup shortening
1 cup milk
1 egg, beaten
⅓ cup brown sugar, firmly packed
1½ teaspoons cinnamon
½ teaspoon salt
¾ teaspoon grated orange rind
2½ tablespoons butter
⅓ cup honey
¾ cup flaked coconut

Sift flour once; measure; add baking powder, salt, and sugar; and sift again. Cut in shortening. Combine milk and egg, and add to flour mixture. Stir with fork until soft dough is formed (about 20 strokes). Turn out onto lightly floured board and knead 30 seconds. Roll out a 15″ x 10″ rectangle, ¼″ thick.

Mix together brown sugar, cinnamon, salt, orange rind, butter, and honey. Spread half of the mixture on dough and sprinkle with half of the coconut. Roll as for jelly roll and cut in 1″ slices. Arrange cut side down in lightly greased muffin tins. Spread top with remaining brown sugar mixture and sprinkle with remaining coconut. Bake at 425° for 20 minutes or until done.

WALNUT HONEY LOAF

1 cup honey
1 cup milk
½ cup sugar
2½ cups sifted flour
1 teaspoon baking soda
1 teaspoon salt
½ cup chopped walnuts
¼ cup shortening
2 egg yolks (or 1 egg)

Combine honey, milk, and sugar in a 3-quart saucepan. Heat over medium heat, stirring constantly, just until sugar is dissolved. (Mixture will be lukewarm.) Set aside to cool.

Sift together the sifted flour, baking soda, and salt. Add to honey mixture together with walnuts, shortening, and egg. Beat for 2 minutes (or 300 strokes) until well blended. Grease and flour (or line with parchment paper) a 9″ x 5″ x 3″ pan. Fill pan and bake at 325° for 75–90 minutes or until done. Cool for 15 minutes, then remove from pan and let cool on wire rack.

Drizzle with a thin glaze, if desired.

The honeybee is one of the oldest forms of life on earth today. It has hardly changed form or lifestyle except to adapt to changing climate and surroundings.

Cakes and Icings

SUPER DELICIOUS CHOCOLATE CAKE

3 squares unsweetened chocolate,
  melted
⅔ cup honey
1¾ cups sifted cake flour
1 teaspoon baking soda
¾ teaspoon salt
½ cup butter or other shortening
½ cup sugar
1 teaspoon vanilla extract
2 eggs, unbeaten
⅔ cup water

FRENCH HONEY CHOCOLATE FROSTING:

½ cup sugar
¼ cup butter
¼ cup light cream
¼ cup honey
¼ teaspoon salt
3 squares unsweetened chocolate, cut
  into small pieces
2 egg yolks, well beaten

Blend chocolate and honey; cool to lukewarm.

Sift flour once, measure, add baking soda and salt, sift together three times.

Cream butter thoroughly, add sugar gradually, and cream together until light and fluffy. Add chocolate/honey mixture and vanilla. Blend. Add eggs, one at a time, beating thoroughly after each addition. Add flour, alternately with water, a small amount at a time, beating after each addition until smooth. Bake in 2 greased and floured 8″ layer pans in 350° oven for 30–35 minutes.

Create frosting by combining sugar, butter, cream, honey, salt, and chocolate in top of double boiler. Place over boiling water. When chocolate is melted, beat with rotary beater until blended. Pour small amount of mixture over egg yolks, stirring vigorously. Return to double boiler and cook 2 minutes longer, or until mixture thickens slightly, stirring constantly. Remove from hot water, place in pan of ice water or cracked ice, and beat until of right consistency to spread over cake.

HONEY ORANGE CAKE

2 cups sifted cake flour
3½ teaspoons baking powder
¾ teaspoon salt
½ cup butter or other shortening
½ cup sugar
⅔ cup honey
2 eggs, separated and whites beaten
½ cup orange juice

Sift flour once, measure, add baking powder and salt, and sift together 3 times.

Cream butter thoroughly, add sugar gradually, and cream together until light and fluffy. Add honey. Blend. Add egg yolks and beat thoroughly. Add flour, alternately with orange juice, a small amount at a time, beating after each addition until smooth. Fold in stiffly beaten egg whites. Bake in 2 greased 9″ layer pans in 350° oven 30–35 minutes.

DELICIOUS VALENTINE CAKE

3 squares unsweetened chocolate, melted
⅔ cup honey
1¾ cups sifted cake flour
1 teaspoon baking soda
¾ teaspoon salt
½ cup butter or other shortening
½ cup sugar
1 teaspoon vanilla extract
2 eggs
⅔ cup water
Flaked coconut
Candy hearts

FLUFFY HONEY MERINGUE:

2 egg whites
Dash of salt
1 cup honey

Blend chocolate and honey; cool to lukewarm.

Sift flour once, measure, add baking soda and salt, and sift together three times.

Cream butter thoroughly, add sugar gradually, and cream together until light and fluffy. Add chocolate/honey mixture and vanilla. Blend. Add eggs, one at a time, beating thoroughly after each addition. Add flour, alternately with water, a small amount at a time, beating after each addition until smooth. Bake in 2 greased 8″ layer pans or heart-shaped pans at 350° for 30–35 minutes.

To create Fluffy Honey Meringue, beat egg whites with salt until stiff enough to hold up in peaks but not dry. Pour honey in fine stream over egg whites, beating constantly until frosting holds its shape (about 10–15 minutes by hand or about 2½ minutes on high speed with an electric mixer). Spread over cake and sprinkle sides with flaked coconut and decorate with candy hearts. This makes a delicious topping for any cake or pudding.

ELEGANT WHITE FRUITCAKE

1 cup cooking oil
1½ cups honey
4 eggs
3 cups sifted flour
1 teaspoon baking powder
¾ teaspoon baking soda
2 teaspoons salt
¾ cup apple juice or pineapple juice
1 pound candied cherries, diced
1 pound candied pineapple, diced
1 pound dates, pitted and cut up
7–8 cups pecans

Mix together cooking oil, honey, and eggs in mixing bowl. Beat 2 minutes.

Sift together 2 cups flour (sifted before measuring), baking powder, baking soda, and salt. Stir in oil/honey mixture alternately with ¾ cup juice.

Combine candied fruit and dust thoroughly with remaining cup of flour. Then pour batter over fruit, mixing well. Line 2 loaf pans or a tube springform pan with parchment paper. Fill with batter. Bake at 275° for 2½–3 hours. Cool before removing from pan. Wrap in foil and store in covered container.

HONEY BUNNY CAKE

½ cup shortening
¾ cup honey
¾ cup milk
1½ teaspoons vanilla extract
¼ teaspoon almond extract
2¼ cups sifted cake flour
3¼ teaspoons baking powder
1 teaspoon salt
¾ cup sugar
4 egg whites, unbeaten

Cream shortening with honey until well blended. Add sifted dry ingredients. Combine milk, vanilla, and almond extract; add ½ cup to flour mixture. Mix until all flour is damp. Beat well. Add egg whites and remaining milk and beat a minute or two longer. Pour batter into 13" x 9" x 2" pan lined with parchment paper. Bake at 350° for 25–30 minutes, or until done.

To make bunny's head, first cut 2 strips from one end of cake, each 1½" wide. These strips are for ears. Remaining piece is for face. Set face piece on large platter or tray, using the longer edges of cake for top and bottom of face. Place the 2 ear strips against top edge of face, slanting them outward slightly.

Frost with Fluffy Honey Meringue (page 98). Spread frosting over top and sides of face and ears. Sprinkle with about 1⅓ cups flaked coconut. If desired, tint some of the coconut pink and sprinkle this along middle of ears. For eyes, nose, and mouth, use jelly beans, gumdrops, or other candies. Twist a licorice stick and use for bow tie.

HONEY LEMON LAYER CAKE

½ cup shortening
1 cup honey
2 eggs
2 cups sifted cake flour
¾ teaspoon baking soda
½ teaspoon salt
¼ cup buttermilk

HONEY CREAM CHEESE FROSTING:

1 three-ounce package cream cheese
1 tablespoon honey
2½ cups sifted confectioners sugar
½ pound lemon fruit candy slices or
  peach slices and cherries

Cream together shortening and honey. Add eggs, one at a time, beating well after each addition.

Sift together flour, baking soda, and salt. Add sifted dry ingredients alternately with buttermilk to egg mixture. Pour into 2 greased 8" layer cake pans. Bake at 350° for 25–30 minutes.

Prepare frosting by blending cheese with honey. Gradually add sugar; beat until smooth.

Frost cake with Honey Cream Cheese Frosting and decorate with lemon candy slices or peaches and cherries.

> In ancient Egypt, honey was offered to the gods, buried in tombs with the dead as food for the hereafter, and given to newborn babies to ward off evil spirits.

ALL-HONEY CHOCOLATE CAKE

2 cups sifted cake flour
1½ teaspoons baking soda
½ teaspoon salt
½ cup shortening
1¼ cups honey
2 eggs
3 squares unsweetened chocolate, melted
⅔ cup water
1 teaspoon vanilla extract

QUICK CREAMED FROSTING:

½ cup honey
½ cup butter
1 teaspoon vanilla extract
2 egg whites
1 cup sifted confectioners sugar
1 square unsweetened chocolate, melted

Sift flour once, measure, add baking soda and salt, and sift together 3 times.

Cream shortening; gradually add honey, beating well after each addition to keep mixture thick. Add one quarter of the flour mixture and beat until smooth and well blended. Add eggs, one at a time, beating well after each. Stir in chocolate and blend. Add remaining flour alternately with water, beating very well after each addition. Add vanilla. Bake in 2 greased, 9″ layer pans at 350° for 30 minutes or until done.

To prepare Quick Creamed Frosting, cream honey and butter. Stir in vanilla. Beat egg whites until they form soft peaks. Add sifted confectioners sugar gradually, beating after each addition. Fold egg white mixture gradually into honey mixture. Add melted chocolate to ⅓ of frosting. Use the chocolate part between the layers. Spread the white frosting on top and sides of cake.

HONEY CHEESECAKE

3 tablespoons butter
2 cups sieved cottage cheese
2 tablespoons sifted flour
1 teaspoon salt
⅓ cup honey
3 tablespoons lemon juice
1 teaspoon lemon rind
4 eggs, separated
⅓ cup sugar
⅔ cup milk

CRUMB BASE:

2 cups crushed graham cracker crumbs
½ cup butter, melted
1 teaspoon cinnamon
⅓ cup honey

Cream butter; blend in cottage cheese, flour, and salt. Beat in honey, lemon juice and rind. Add egg yolks, one at a time, beating well after each addition.

Beat egg whites until stiff. Slowly add sugar; beat until soft peaks form. Fold into cheese mixture. Blend in milk.

Combine all ingredients for Crumb Base. Press all but ½ cup mixture firmly along bottom and sides of 11½″ x 7½″ x 1½″ pan. Pour in filling and sprinkle with remaining crumb mixture. Bake about 350° about 1 hour. Chill for easier cutting.

HONEY UPSIDE-DOWN CAKE WITH HONEY SAUCE

BOTTOM LAYER:

½ cup honey
¼ cup butter
4 or 5 unpeeled apples
Pecan halves
Maraschino cherries

BATTER:

½ cup butter
¾ cup honey
1 egg
½ cup milk
1½ cups flour
1 teaspoon baking powder
¼ teaspoon baking soda
¼ teaspoon cinnamon
½ teaspoon nutmeg
⅛ teaspoon ground ginger

HONEY SAUCE:

½ cup honey
½ cup butter

Put ½ cup honey and ¼ cup butter in a heavy, medium-sized iron skillet and let slowly melt on top of stove. Core the unpeeled apples and cut them crosswise into ring slices ¾" thick, preparing enough slices to cover bottom of skillet. Add the apple rings to honey and butter and simmer until apples are partly cooked, turning once. Place a maraschino cherry in center of each apple ring, and pecan halves in the spaces around the apples.

Prepare the batter by creaming together butter and honey; add egg and beat until smooth. Add milk alternately with sifted dry ingredients.

Pour this batter over the hot fruit layer. Bake in heavy skillet at 350° 30–35 minutes. Turn upside-down cake onto a large platter. This may be served hot or cold. Serve with Honey Sauce.

To prepare Honey Sauce, heat honey with melted butter; stir to combine.

MERINGUE SPICE CAKE

¾ cup shortening
1 cup brown sugar, firmly packed
1 cup honey
2 egg yolks, beaten
2⅓ cups flour
¾ teaspoon salt
2 teaspoons baking powder
1 teaspoon baking soda
1 teaspoon cinnamon
1 teaspoon ground cloves
1 cup sour milk
1 teaspoon vanilla extract

BROWN SUGAR MERINGUE:

2 egg whites, stiffly beaten
1 cup brown sugar, firmly packed
½ cup broken nut meats

Thoroughly cream shortening, brown sugar, and honey; add egg yolks and beat until fluffy. Add sifted dry ingredients, alternating with milk and vanilla. Beat vigorously after each addition. Pour into greased 9" x 13" cake pan.

Prepare meringue by slowly adding sugar and nuts to egg whites and beat until smooth. Spread over batter and bake at 325° about 50 minutes.

CHOICE HONEY FRUITCAKE

3 cups sifted flour
1 teaspoon salt
1½ teaspoons baking soda
½ teaspoon cinnamon
½ teaspoon mace
½ teaspoon allspice
3 cups raisins
3½ cups currants
½ pound or 1¼ cups red and green
    candied cherries, sliced
1 cup chopped walnuts or pecans
½ cup heavy fruit syrup or sweetened
    juice
6 tablespoons white vinegar
1 cup shortening
1 cup honey
¼ cup brown sugar, firmly packed
6 eggs, beaten

Sift together 2½ cups flour, salt, baking soda, and spices.

Steam raisins and currants over boiling water, spread on paper towels and let dry until quite cool. Combine raisins, currants, cherries, and nuts with remaining ½ cup of flour.

Combine fruit syrup or sweetened juice and vinegar.

Cream together the shortening, honey, and brown sugar; beat until light and creamy. Beat in eggs. Add dry ingredients and liquids alternately, a little of each at a time, stirring in after each addition just enough to blend well. Stir in fruits and nuts.

Pour into a 10″ tube pan which has been lined with parchment paper. Bake at 300° for 3 hours.

If you prefer, cake may be baked in a long angel food pan (15½″ x 4½″ x 4½″) about 2½ hours.

OLD-FASHIONED HONEY CAKE

1 cup butter
1 cup sugar
3 eggs
1 teaspoon baking soda
1 cup honey
3 cups sifted flour
1 teaspoon baking powder
1 teaspoon cinnamon
½ teaspoon ground ginger
¼ teaspoon nutmeg
¼ teaspoon ground cloves
1 cup milk

Cream butter and sugar, beat in eggs.

Add baking soda to honey.

Sift all dry ingredients together.

Add honey and milk alternately with dry ingredients to creamed mixture. Blend well. Bake in a 13″ x 9″ x 2″ pan in a 350° oven for 45–50 minutes. Delicious with a quickie topping of honey drizzled over hot cake and sprinkled with a mixture of sugar and cinnamon.

North American Indians believed that honeybees brought misfortune, and called them white man's flies, because when bees arrived, it meant that settlers had also come.

SPICE CAKE WITH BANANAS AND HONEY CUSTARD SAUCE

1 package of spice cake mix
2 ripe bananas

HONEY CUSTARD SAUCE:

2 eggs
⅓ cup honey
⅛ teaspoon salt
1⅔ cups evaporated milk (1 tall can)
1 cup boiling water
½ teaspoon vanilla extract
⅛ teaspoon nutmeg

Prepare cake mix according to package directions and bake in 8″ x 12″ baking pan.

To prepare Honey Custard Sauce, beat eggs in top of double boiler. Add honey and salt. Blend well, then add milk. Stir in the boiling water. Cook over boiling water, stirring constantly until mixture just coats a spoon, about 4–5 minutes. Remove from heat immediately and place top of double boiler in cold water to hasten cooling and keep mixture from further cooking. Stir frequently while cooling. Add vanilla and nutmeg. Makes about 3 cups sauce.

Cake may be served slightly warm or cold, with sliced bananas on top, and topped with Honey Custard Sauce.

CHOCOLATE BUTTERCREAM ICING

1¾ cups powdered sugar
¾ cup cocoa
¼ teaspoon salt
3 tablespoons butter
3 tablespoons shortening
1 tablespoon honey
1 egg white
2 tablespoons milk

Sift dry ingredients together and place in mixing bowl with remaining ingredients except milk. Mix until smooth. Add milk and mix at low speed until light.

CHOCOLATE FUDGE ICING

1¾ cups powdered sugar
¾ cup cocoa
¼ teaspoon salt
3 tablespoons butter
2 tablespoons shortening
1½ tablespoons honey
1 egg white
2–3 tablespoons hot milk

Have all ingredients at room temperature. Sift dry ingredients together. Mix in warmed bowl with remainder of ingredients, except milk, until smooth. Add hot milk and mix until smooth. Keep in warm bowl (115°) until used, stirring occasionally. Too high a temperature causes icing to lose its shine.

COOKIES AND DESSERTS

GERMAN HONEY COOKIES

3 ounces each citron, candied orange
   peel, and candied lemon peel
1 cup chopped blanched almonds, plus
   some for decorating
1 teaspoon grated lemon rind
3 tablespoons cinnamon
1 tablespoon cloves
3⅓ cups powdered sugar
6 eggs, beaten until light
¼ cup orange juice
2 cups honey
2 tablespoons hot water
5 cups sifted flour
1 tablespoon baking soda

LEMON OR ORANGE GLAZE:

1¼ cups confectioners sugar
¼ cup lemon or orange juice

Cut citron and candied peels into small pieces and combine. Add chopped almonds, lemon rind, cinnamon, cloves, and powdered sugar. Add beaten eggs and orange juice, beating until smooth.

Heat honey and the 2 tablespoons hot water until it just reaches the boiling point. Cool until lukewarm. Then stir honey into egg mixture and stir in flour and baking soda.

Cover the dough and let stand in refrigerator or where it is cool for 12 hours or more. Drop by spoonful, well apart, on a greased baking sheet. Bake at 350° for 12–18 minutes or until light brown.

Prepare glaze by thoroughly mixing juice and sugar. Spread on warm cookies. Top with almonds if desired. Makes about 200, 2½" cookies.

HONEYBEE DIAMONDS

¾ cup butter
¾ cup sugar
3 eggs
1 cup sifted flour
1½ teaspoons baking powder
¼ teaspoon salt
½ teaspoon cinnamon
¼ cup milk
1 teaspoon grated orange peel
1 cup chopped walnuts

HONEY SYRUP:

1 cup honey
½ cup water
¼ cup sugar
1 tablespoon lemon juice

Cream butter and sugar; add eggs, one at a time, beating well after each addition.

Sift together flour, baking powder, salt, and cinnamon; add to batter. Stir in milk and orange peel. Beat well and blend in nuts. Pour into a greased and floured 9" x 13" pan. Bake at 350° for 30 minutes or until done. Remove from oven.

To prepare Honey Syrup, simmer honey, water, and sugar together for 5 minutes. Skim and add lemon juice; simmer 2 additional minutes. Cool. Pour syrup over cookies; refrigerate. Cut into diamonds to serve. Makes 2 dozen cookies.

> *In some ancient cultures, honey was considered so valuable that it was sometimes used in place of gold to pay taxes.*

HONEY RAISIN BARS

DOUGH:

1¼ cups sifted flour
3 tablespoons sugar
1 teaspoon baking powder
¼ teaspoon salt
½ cup butter or margarine
1 tablespoon water
1 teaspoon grated orange peel
1 egg

FILLING:

1 tablespoon water
2 teaspoons grated orange peel
1 egg
½ cup honey
2 tablespoons soft butter or margarine
¾ cup raisins, chopped
¾ cup shredded moist coconut
½ cup chopped pecans

HONEY GLAZE:

2 tablespoons honey
1 tablespoon soft butter or margarine
1 tablespoon water
½ teaspoon orange extract
1 cup confectioners sugar

To make the dough, sift together the flour, sugar, baking powder, and salt. Cut in the butter with a pastry blender until particles are fine.

Combine water, orange peel, and egg. Beat with a rotary beater until light. Add to flour mixture, stirring with fork until dough is moist enough to hold together.

Roll out half of the dough on a piece of waxed paper to make a 9″ square. Invert into an ungreased 9″ square pan, remove paper, and pat dough in place. Press any extra edges up sides of pan. Roll out remainder of dough on waxed paper, same size; set aside.

To make filling, combine water, orange peel, and egg. Beat together with a fork. Add honey, butter, chopped raisins, coconut, and chopped pecans. Spread over dough in pan. Place remaining dough over filling. Press down lightly; remove paper. Dip fork tines in flour and prick top. Bake in a 375° oven 25–35 minutes or until top is lightly browned.

Let cool 10–15 minutes. To make Honey Glaze, combine honey, butter, water, orange extract, and confectioners sugar. Beat until smooth. Spread over top of uncut cookies. Cool completely before cutting into bars. Makes 2 dozen.

HONEY NUT COOKIES

2 egg whites
½ cup honey
½ cup sugar
¼ teaspoon salt
¼ cup water
1 tablespoon flavoring
1 cup chopped black walnuts

Beat egg whites with rotary beater until stiff. Gradually add honey, beating after each addition. Continue beating until mixture is stiff.

Combine sugar, salt, and water in small saucepan. Cook until sugar is dissolved and mixture boils, stirring constantly. Cover tightly and boil 2 minutes. Uncover and boil, without stirring, until a small amount of syrup forms a firm ball in cold water (250°).

Pour syrup in fine stream over egg mixture, beating constantly. Beat until cool and thickened. Add nuts and flavoring. Drop from teaspoon on well-buttered and floured baking sheet. Bake at 300° for 25–30 minutes or until delicately browned. Carefully remove from sheet with sharp edge of clean knife.

GLAZED CHRISTMAS COOKIES

2 cups sifted flour
1 teaspoon baking soda
1 teaspoon salt
½ cup soft butter or margarine
1 teaspoon vanilla extract
½ teaspoon almond extract
⅔ cup honey
1 egg, well beaten
¼ cup vinegar
½ cup finely cut mixed candied peel
½ cup finely cut red or green candied
    cherries
½ cup finely cut shredded coconut
1 egg white, lightly beaten
Red sanding sugar
Split, blanched almonds

Sift together flour, baking soda, and salt.

Cream together butter or margarine, vanilla and almond extracts, and honey; beat until fluffy and creamy. Beat in egg and vinegar. Stir in sifted dry ingredients gradually; blend well. Mix in candied peel, cherries, and coconut.

Chill dough several hours or overnight. Shape one quarter of the dough at a time, leaving remaining dough

in refrigerator. Shape into balls ¾" in diameter. Place 2" apart on greased cookie sheet.

Grease the bottom of a 2" diameter glass tumbler, then dip in flour. Press cookies with tumbler, dipping tumbler in flour as needed. Brush surface of cookies with lightly beaten egg white; sprinkle with red sugar.

Arrange split blanched almonds in flower petal pattern on each. Bake in a 375° oven about 12 minutes. Remove from pan immediately. Makes about 6 dozen cookies.

HONEY OATMEAL CHEWS

½ cup butter
½ cup honey
½ cup sugar
1 egg
1 teaspoon vanilla extract
⅔ cup sifted flour
½ teaspoon baking soda
½ teaspoon baking powder
¼ teaspoon salt
1 cup quick-cooking oats
1 cup flaked coconut
½ cup chopped almonds

Cream butter, honey, and sugar until light and fluffy. Add egg and vanilla; beat well.

Sift together flour, baking soda, baking powder, and salt. Add to creamed mixture. Stir in oats, coconut, and nuts. Spread in a greased 9" x 13" baking pan. Bake at 350° for 20–25 minutes. When cool, cut into bars about 1½" x 2½". Makes 30 bars.

FRUITCAKE COOKIES

1 cup sifted flour
½ teaspoon baking soda
¼ teaspoon salt
½ teaspoon cinnamon
½ teaspoon cloves
½ teaspoon allspice
⅛ teaspoon nutmeg
¼ cup shortening
½ cup honey
¼ cup brown sugar, firmly packed
1 egg, beaten
2 tablespoons milk
2 tablespoons vinegar
¼ teaspoon imitation rum extract
¼ teaspoon vanilla extract
½ cup raisins
½ cup currants
½ cup finely cut candied pineapple
½ cup finely cut candied citron
¾ cup sliced candied cherries
¾ cup coarsely chopped pecans

DECORATION:

Confectioners sugar
Cherries
Cinnamon red hots
Colored sugar

Sift together flour, baking soda, salt, and spices.

Cream together shortening, honey, and brown sugar; beat until light and creamy. Beat in egg, milk, vinegar, rum and vanilla extracts. Stir in dry ingredients gradually. Mix in fruits and nuts.

Drop from tip of teaspoon onto greased baking sheet. Bake in 325° oven about 20 minutes. Remove from pan immediately.

When cooled, frost with confectioners sugar frosting and garnish with red hots, candied cherries, or colored sugar. Makes 4 dozen cookies.

POINSETTIA BALLS

3 cups sifted flour
½ teaspoon baking soda
½ teaspoon salt
1 cup butter or margarine
⅔ cup honey
2 tablespoons grated orange rind
2 eggs, separated
1 tablespoon grated lemon rind
2 tablespoons white vinegar
1½ cups finely chopped pecans
7 dozen red candied cherries

Sift together flour, baking soda, and salt.

Cream together butter or margarine and honey; beat until light and creamy. Beat in egg yolks until well blended. Beat in orange and lemon rinds and vinegar until well blended. Stir in dry ingredients gradually; mix well. Chill dough for 1 hour.

Form into balls about 1″ in diameter. Beat egg whites lightly. Dip balls in egg whites, then roll in pecans. Place 2″ apart on greased baking sheet. Cut each cherry with scissors from top almost to bottom in thin slices to form petals. Place a cut cherry on top of each ball, spreading cherry petals into a flower. Bake in 325° oven for 18–20 minutes. Makes 7 dozen cookies.

> In Roman mythology, Amor, the god of love, dipped his arrows in honey.

HONEY DATE PUDDING WITH LEMON SAUCE

¼ cup butter
1 cup honey
2 eggs
½ teaspoon vanilla extract
2½ cups cake flour, sifted
2½ teaspoons baking powder
½ teaspoon cinnamon
½ teaspoon ground cloves
½ teaspoon nutmeg
½ teaspoon salt
¾ cup chopped dates
½ cup pecan pieces
1 cup evaporated milk

LEMON SAUCE:

2 tablespoons cornstarch
1¾ cups water
¾ cup honey
1 egg, well beaten
¼ teaspoon salt
¼ cup lemon juice
2 teaspoons grated lemon peel

Cream butter until light and fluffy. Add honey, eggs, and vanilla; beat 1 minute.

Sift together flour, baking powder, cinnamon, cloves, nutmeg, and salt; add dates and nuts; and mix until dates are flour coated. Add milk to flour mixture; stir until well blended.

Combine both mixtures; pour into buttered 5-cup mold. Cover tightly with lid that fits mold or with foil tied with strong cord. Place in pressure cooker on rack. Pour in hot water to come halfway up side of mold. Close cooker lid tightly; start cooker on high heat. Let steam escape for 30 minutes. Place pressure regulator on vent pipe; when regulator begins to rock gently, cook for an additional 45 minutes at medium heat. Remove cooker from heat and set in cool water. When pressure drops, remove regulator. Remove pudding; take off lid or foil. Cool slightly; remove pudding from mold.

Note: If pudding is steamed on a rack in a steamer or large kettle, steam for 2 hours.

To create Lemon Sauce, mix cornstarch with small amount of water. Add remaining water; honey, egg, and salt and blend well. Cook and stir until mixture thickens and comes to a boil. Remove from heat; stir in lemon juice and peel. Serve over pudding.

HONEY RAISIN PIE

1½ cups raisins
1 tablespoon grated orange rind
1 cup orange juice
¼ cup lemon juice
¾ cup honey
2 tablespoons butter
½ teaspoon salt
¼ cup cornstarch
¾ cup cold water
Pastry for double crust (9″)

Combine raisins, orange rind and juice, lemon juice, honey, butter, salt, and cornstarch that has been moistened in the cold water, and stir until blended.

Bring to a boil; cook and stir until mixture thickens (3 or 4 minutes). Pour into pastry-lined pie pan, cover with top crust. Bake at 425° for 30–35 minutes. Cool before serving.

PUMPKIN PIE

¾ cup strained honey
¾ cup nonfat dry milk
½ teaspoon salt
½ teaspoon cinnamon
½ teaspoon mace
½ teaspoon ground ginger
¼ teaspoon ground cloves
1½ cups cooked pumpkin
2 eggs, well beaten
1½ cups water
2 tablespoons melted butter
1 unbaked 9" pastry shell

Mix dry ingredients well to prevent streaking. Add other ingredients. Blend thoroughly. Turn into pastry shell. Bake at 425° for 15 minutes. Reduce to 350° and bake 40 minutes longer.

CRANBERRY PUDDING

2 cups large cranberries, cut in half
1½ cups flour
⅔ cup honey
⅓ cup hot water
1 teaspoon baking soda
½ teaspoon salt
½ teaspoon baking powder

HONEY SAUCE:

½ cup butter
⅔ cup honey
2 tablespoons flour
2 eggs, lightly beaten
½ cup lemon juice
½ pint whipping cream

Mix cranberries with the flour, then add in other dry ingredients. Mix honey with hot water and add to mix-

ture. Put all in steamer and steam 2 hours. Serve with Honey Sauce.

To Prepare Honey Sauce, mix and cook first 4 ingredients slowly in double boiler until thickened. Remove from heat. Add lemon juice. When cool and ready to serve, whip cream and fold in.

HONEY RICE PUDDING

⅔ cup minute rice
1 cup water
¼ teaspoon salt
1¼ cups milk
1 egg yolk, lightly beaten
½ cup honey
⅛ teaspoon nutmeg
⅛ teaspoon cinnamon
1 tablespoon butter
⅓ cup raisins
Honey
Whipping cream

Combine rice, water, and salt in saucepan. Bring to a boil, cover, and boil gently 4 minutes, or until water is absorbed. Remove from heat.

Combine milk and egg yolk; add to rice in saucepan and blend. Add honey, spices, butter, and raisins; mix well. Bring again to a boil, stirring constantly. Cover; remove from heat. Cool to room temperature. Serve with honey-sweetened whipped cream.

> A pharaoh who lived more than 2000 years before the Exodus is believed to have introduced the honeybee into Egypt.

HONEY DELIGHT

*1 package lemon- or orange-flavored
gelatin*
½ cup boiling water
½ cup honey
Juice of ½ lemon
*1 can evaporated milk, chilled and
whipped*
½ pound vanilla wafers, crushed

Dissolve gelatin in boiling water. Add honey and lemon juice and mix well. Fold in evaporated milk. Pour this mixture into a pan that has been lined with crushed vanilla wafers, reserving some for topping. Place crushed vanilla wafers on top of mixture and put in refrigerator to set. Cut into squares.

RHUBARB AND PEACH HONEY COBBLER

1 pound quick-frozen rhubarb, thawed
*10 ounces quick-frozen sliced peaches,
thawed*
1½ tablespoons quick-cooking tapioca
⅔ cup honey
1 cup sifted flour
1½ teaspoons baking powder
2 tablespoons sugar
½ teaspoon salt
¼ teaspoon mace or nutmeg
⅓ cup butter or other shortening
¼ cup milk
Honey-sweetened whipped cream

Drain the rhubarb and peaches, reserving the juices. Combine juices with tapioca and bring to a boil, stirring constantly. Add honey. Remove from heat. Add rhubarb and peaches to the thickened juice. Pour into 2-quart baking dish.

Sift flour once; measure; add baking powder, sugar, salt, and nutmeg; and sift again. Cut in shortening. Add milk gradually, stirring until a soft dough is formed. Turn out on lightly floured board and knead 10 seconds or enough to shape. Pat or roll dough to fit top of baking dish. Cut several slits in center and adjust dough over fruit mixture, opening slits with knife to permit escape of steam. Bake in 400° oven 30 minutes. Serve hot or cold, with honey-sweetened whipped cream.

HONEY PECAN PIE

1 cup strained honey
3 well-beaten eggs
2 tablespoons sugar
¼ cup nonfat dry milk
¼ cup butter
1½ cups chopped pecans
½ teaspoon vanilla extract
1 unbaked 9″ pastry shell

Mix honey with well-beaten eggs. Cream sugar, nonfat dry milk, butter, and add to honey/egg mixture. Stir in pecans and vanilla. Turn into an unbaked 9″ crust and bake at 375° for 1 hour or until center tests done with knife.

VARIATION:

For small tarts, muffin tins may be lined with rounds of pastry and each filled with 1 teaspoon of the above mixture. Bake 10–12 minutes at 425°.

FRENCH APPLE DUMPLING

2 cups flour
4 teaspoons baking powder
½ teaspoon salt
¼ cup shortening
¾ cup milk
4 large apples, sliced
½ cup sugar
¼ teaspoon cinnamon
Melted butter

HONEY DUMPLING SAUCE:

1½ cups honey
2 tablespoons cornstarch
1½ cups water
⅛ teaspoon salt
1 tablespoon butter
½ teaspoon vanilla extract

Mix first five ingredients as for biscuit dough. Handle as lightly as possible. Roll out the dough ¼″ thick on a floured towel.

Cover the dough with the sliced apples and sprinkle with sugar and cinnamon. Roll like a jelly roll and cut into 1″ slices. Place slices in a buttered baking pan. Put 1 teaspoon melted butter over each roll. Bake at 400° for 20–25 minutes. Serve with Honey Dumpling Sauce.

To prepare Honey Dumpling Sauce, mix all ingredients except vanilla and cook until clear. Add ½ teaspoon vanilla. Serve on the hot slices.

It takes 556 worker bees flying the equivalent of 1⅓ times around the world to produce just one pound of honey.

HONEY PUMPKIN CHIFFON PIE

GRAHAM CRACKER CRUST:

20 graham crackers (1⅔ cups crumbs)
¼ cup sifted confectioners sugar
¼ cup soft butter

FILLING:

1 tablespoon unflavored gelatin
¼ cup cold water
3 eggs, separated
¾ cup honey
2 cups cooked pumpkin
½ cup whole milk
½ teaspoon salt
1 teaspoon cinnamon
½ teaspoon ground ginger
¼ teaspoon ground cloves
3 tablespoons sugar
½ pint whipping cream, whipped

Crush the graham crackers very fine. Blend in the sugar and soft butter. Press the mixture into a heat-resistant, deep 10″ pie dish. Bake at 375° for 10 minutes.

Soak gelatin in cold water 5 minutes. Beat egg yolks and combine with honey, pumpkin, milk, salt, and spices. Cook in top of double boiler until thick, stirring constantly. Remove from heat, add softened gelatin, and stir until dissolved.

Beat egg whites until frothy; add sugar gradually and continue beating until they stand in peaks. Fold into pumpkin mixture. Turn into graham crust and chill for several hours. Top with whipped cream.

Honey Berry Float

1 quart milk, chilled
6 tablespoons honey
2 cups crushed fresh strawberries
½ teaspoon almond extract
1 quart vanilla ice cream

Combine milk, honey, strawberries, almond extract, and one pint ice cream. Beat with rotary beater until blended. Pour into tall glasses and garnish with scoops of ice cream.

Honeycomb Pie

PASTRY:

1 cup sifted flour
⅛ teaspoon grated lemon rind
½ teaspoon salt
¼ teaspoon sugar
¼ cup shortening
2 tablespoons butter
2–3 tablespoons cold water

FILLING:

¾ cup sifted flour
¼ teaspoon salt
1 teaspoon baking soda
1 cup sugar
3 eggs
½ cup butter, melted
⅓ cup milk
¼ cup lemon juice
½ teaspoon grated lemon rind
1 cup honey
Whipped cream

Toss together flour, lemon rind, salt, and sugar in mixing bowl. Cut shortening and butter in with pastry blender or blending fork until pieces are size of rice kernels. Sprinkle water evenly over mixture and toss with fork until evenly dampened. Roll on floured board or pastry cloth into a 10" circle. Line a 9" pie plate with pastry, flute edge. Chill.

Prepare filling by sifting together flour, salt, and baking soda; add sugar; toss together lightly.

Beat eggs until thick and lemon colored; beat in butter, milk, lemon juice and rind, and honey; blend well.

Add dry ingredients; blend well. Pour into chilled, unbaked pie shell. Bake in a 325° oven for 55–60 minutes. Cool on cake rack. Chill before serving. Serve with whipped cream.

Baked Bananas with Honey

4 firm bananas (use all-yellow or
    slightly green-tipped bananas)
2 tablespoons melted butter or
    margarine
Honey

Peel bananas. Place in a well-greased baking dish. Brush bananas with honey so that entire banana is covered. Bake at 350° for 15–20 minutes, or until bananas are tender (easily pierced with a fork). Remove from oven. With tip of spoon make a shallow groove running the length of each banana. Fill each groove with about ½ teaspoon honey.

RHUBARB TARTS

2 cups rhubarb, washed and cut in ½"
  pieces
2 eggs, separated
¾ cup honey
3 tablespoons flour
¼ teaspoon salt
2 tablespoons honey

Pour boiling water over the rhubarb and drain in colander.

Mix egg yolks (lightly beaten), ¾ cup honey, flour, and salt. Add to rhubarb. Pour into pastry-lined muffin pans. Bake at 350° for 30 minutes or until done. Top with meringue made by adding 2 tablespoons honey to 2 stiffly beaten egg whites.

HONEY CRUNCH CRUST

1 cup flaked coconut, toasted
1 cup honey-flavored puffed wheat
¼ cup honey
2 tablespoons granulated sugar
¼ teaspoon salt
1 tablespoon butter

Place coconut and cereal in a greased bowl and set aside.

Combine honey, sugar, and salt in a small saucepan. Bring to a boil over medium heat, stirring to dissolve sugar. Continue boiling until small amount of syrup forms a firm ball in cold water (or to a temperature of 246°). Add butter. Pour syrup over coconut and cereal in bowl, stirring lightly to coat. Press mixture on bottom and sides of well-greased 9" pie pan. Chill.

HONEY ICE CREAM PIE

1 Honey Crunch Crust (or a baked pie
  shell)
1½ quarts of ice cream
1⅓ cups flaked coconut, toasted
Honey

Soften the ice cream slightly and fold in 1 cup of flaked coconut. Fill the prepared pie shell with scoops of the ice cream. Drizzle honey over the top, and sprinkle on the remaining flaked coconut.

TAPIOCA CREAM

⅓ cup quick-cooking tapioca
⅓ cup honey
¼ teaspoon salt
2 eggs, separated and whites beaten
4 cups milk, scalded
1 teaspoon vanilla extract

Combine tapioca, honey, salt, and egg yolks in top of double boiler. Add milk slowly and mix thoroughly. Cook until tapioca is transparent, stirring often. Remove from the heat and fold into the stiffly beaten egg whites. Add the vanilla. This may be served either warm or cold with cream.

A scotch whiskey base, honey, and special herbs and spices result in the crown jewel of all liqueurs—Drambuie.

HONEY COCONUT ICE CREAM

1 cup honey
1 envelope unflavored gelatin
2 tablespoons cold water
¼ cup brown sugar, firmly packed
2 eggs
3 cups light cream
1 teaspoon coconut extract or ½
    teaspoon almond extract
½ cup flaked or shredded coconut

Heat honey (do not boil). Soften gelatin in water; add to honey along with sugar, eggs, cream, and extract. Beat about 2 minutes. Pour into refrigerator tray. Freeze until firm, but not hard. Turn mixture into chilled bowl. Beat until fluffy. Pour back into refrigerator tray and freeze until firm. Toast coconut; sprinkle over each serving.

HONEY CUSTARD

¼ teaspoon salt
3 eggs, lightly beaten
¼ cup honey
2 cups milk, scalded
Nutmeg

Add salt to eggs. Beat eggs just long enough to combine whites and yolks. Add honey to milk. Add honey and milk mixture slowly to eggs. Pour into custard cups. Top with a few gratings of nutmeg. Set custard cups in pan of hot water. Bake at 325° about 40 minutes or until custard is firm.

HONEY-BAKED PEARS

Wash, halve, and core pears.

In a baking dish, put the juice of half a lemon and enough water to cover bottom of pan. Place the pears, cut side down, in dish and bake covered at 375° for 20 minutes. At the end of this time, remove, cover, and turn pears. Drizzle pears with honey, allowing about 2 teaspoons honey per pear half. Return to oven to complete baking and to glaze pears, about 10–15 minutes.

Serve as a meat accompaniment or as dessert with fresh cream, commercial sour cream, or whipped cream, allowing 1 large half or 2 small halves per serving.

MEATS AND VEGETABLES

HONEY HAM LOAF

2 pounds ground ham
1 pound ground fresh pork
3 slices bread
½ cup milk
2 eggs
¼ cup honey
½ teaspoon cinnamon
½ teaspoon cloves

TOPPING:

¼ cup brown sugar, firmly packed
¼ cup honey
2 tablespoons vinegar

Combine ground meats in mixing bowl. Soak bread in milk and add to meat with remaining ingredients. Mix thoroughly. Mold into loaf and place in shallow roasting pan. Before baking, combine topping ingredients and spread over top of loaf. Bake in 350° oven for 2 hours.

HONEY-GLAZED DUCKLING

5-pound duckling
1 teaspoon salt
1 teaspoon seasoned salt
1 teaspoon poultry seasoning
½ teaspoon paprika
½ cup honey
⅓ cup orange and lemon juice
1 teaspoon dry mustard
5 thin slices lemon
5 thin slices onion

Clean duck and prick skin to allow fat to drain off when cooking. Combine salt, seasoned salt, poultry seasoning, and paprika and rub inside and outside of duck. Place duck on rack in shallow pan. Place in 450° oven for 15 minutes; drain off fat. Reduce oven temperature to 350° and bake for 1 hour, draining fat as necessary. Combine honey, orange and lemon juice with mustard and brush duck with it. Secure sliced lemon and onion on duck with toothpicks, bake for 45 minutes more, brushing frequently with honey glaze.

OVEN-FRIED CHICKEN WITH HONEY BUTTER SAUCE

2½–3 pound broiler cut up for frying
1 cup flour
2 teaspoons salt
¼ teaspoon pepper
2 teaspoons paprika
½ cup butter

HONEY BUTTER SAUCE:

¼ cup melted butter
¼ cup honey
¼ cup lemon juice

Dip chicken pieces into mixture of flour, salt, pepper, and paprika.

Melt butter in a shallow baking pan in hot oven. Remove baking pan from oven. As pieces of floured chicken are placed in pan, turn to coat with butter, then bake skin side down in a single layer. Bake at 400° for 30 minutes. Turn chicken.

Prepare Honey Butter Sauce by melting butter and beating in honey and lemon juice. Pour Honey Butter Sauce over chicken. Bake another 30 minutes, or until tender. Spoon Honey Butter Sauce over chicken again.

HONEY-FRUITED PORK CHOPS

4 double-thick pork loin chops
8½ ounce can sliced pineapple, drained
    and ¼ cup syrup reserved
½ cup honey
1 tablespoon prepared mustard
Maraschino cherries

Cut a pocket into each chop and insert a half slice of pineapple. Combine honey, pineapple syrup, and mustard; spoon a little over each chop. Bake at 350° for 1½ hours, drizzling honey sauce over the chops frequently.

Remove chops from oven; top each with a half slice of pineapple and a maraschino cherry. Return to oven for a minute or two to warm the fruit. Heat any remaining honey sauce and serve with chops.

MARINATED FLANK STEAK

Two 1½ pound flank steaks
¼ cup soy sauce
3 tablespoons honey
2 tablespoons red wine vinegar
1½ teaspoons garlic powder
1½ teaspoons ground ginger
¾ cup salad oil
1 finely chopped green onion

Combine soy sauce, honey, and vinegar in a mixing bottle or jar with a tight lid. Add garlic powder and ginger. Then add salad oil and onion and mix well.

Prepare meat by stripping off excess fat. Slash lightly on the diagonal (on each side) in diamond-shaped cuts.

Place meat in a small pan just big enough to hold it. Pour marinade over. Cover. Allow to stand at room temperature 2 hours, or place in the refrigerator overnight.

When ready to cook, remove steak from marinade and place on grill using medium heat. This meat cooks fast: about 6 minutes per side for medium rare.

To serve, slice thinly on the diagonal. Serves 4.

May also be served on buns as sandwiches.

BARBECUED SPARERIBS

4 pounds spareribs

BARBECUE SAUCE:
½ cup chopped onion
2 garlic cloves
1½ cups ketchup
2 tablespoons vinegar
½ teaspoon salt
1 teaspoon prepared mustard
½ teaspoon black pepper
2 tablespoons thick steak sauce
1 cup strained honey

Cut spareribs into serving portions. Place in enough water to cover. Add 2 teaspoons salt, simmer for ½ hour.

For the sauce, mix the remaining ingredients and cook over low heat for 5–7 minutes. Drain spareribs and place in shallow baking pan. Pour barbecue sauce over ribs and bake in 400° oven for 45 minutes or until tender. Baste every 10 minutes with sauce.

BAKED SLICED HAM WITH HONEY GLAZE

1 canned ham (5–6 pounds)
Whole cloves

HONEY GLAZE:

¼ cup honey
¼ cup ketchup
2 tablespoons prepared mustard
2 teaspoons minced onion
2 teaspoons Worcestershire sauce
¼ teaspoon grated lemon peel
⅛ teaspoon ginger

Have ham pre-sliced and tied securely together with string. Keep refrigerated until ready to bake. Press cloves in rows or in pattern in top of ham slices. Place on rack in shallow baking pan.

To prepare Honey Glaze, mix together honey, ketchup, mustard, onion, Worcestershire sauce, lemon peel, and ginger. Spread over top and sides of ham. Bake in a 350° oven about 1 hour. Serve hot or cold. May be garnished with drained canned pineapple slices and pitted cooked prunes.

GARNISH AND GLAZE FOR BAKED HAM

1 ham
1 cup strained honey
2 large oranges
4 slices canned pineapple, syrup
    reserved
Whole cloves

One hour before ham is done, remove rind, score fat in large squares, and cover with ½ cup honey. Let bake until glazed and lightly browned.

Wash oranges, score the rind in 4 equal sections and remove carefully. With small star-shaped cutter, cut star from each section of rind. Remove as much of inner white portion as possible. Divide pulp into sections and remove fibrous covering. Place orange peel stars, orange sections, and half slices of pineapple in pan with remaining honey and let cook until fruit is glazed and peel is tender. Just before ham is done, fasten a star in each square of fat with a long-stemmed clove, and baste with honey and fruit syrup. Garnish platter with glazed fruit and crisp parsley.

HONEY MINT SAUCE FOR LAMB

½ cup water
1 tablespoon vinegar
1 cup honey
¼ cup chopped mint

Heat water and vinegar. Add honey, stir well, then add chopped mint. Cook slowly for 5 minutes. This sauce can be used to baste lamb chops or lamb roast during cooking or can be served with meat at the table.

Possibly the earliest proof of man's use of honey is a prehistoric painting found in Valencia, Spain, and estimated to be approximately 15,000 years old. The painting shows a woman gathering honey from a hole in a cliff.

HONEY-BAKED SQUASH

1 acorn squash
4 or 6 small pork links
4 teaspoons honey

Wash squash, cut in half, and remove seeds. Place 2 teaspoons honey in each half. Also place 2 or 3 cooked and drained pork links in each half. Bake at 350° for 30–40 minutes or until squash is done.

CITRUS HONEY CARROTS

1 bunch carrots
Salt
¼ cup melted butter or margarine
¼ cup honey
1½ teaspoons grated orange peel
1½ teaspoons grated lemon peel

Wash and scrape carrots; cook in 1" of boiling salted water until crisp but tender, about 15–20 minutes. Drain. Blend melted butter, honey, and citrus peels. Pour over cooked carrots and place over low heat until carrots are thoroughly glazed.

CANDIED SWEET POTATOES

Boil 6 medium-sized, whole sweet potatoes. When tender, drain and remove skins. Cut in half lengthwise and arrange in buttered baking dish. Season with salt. Heat ¼ cup butter, ½ cup honey, and ½ cup orange juice, and pour over potatoes. Bake at 400° until potatoes are brown.

HONEY-BAKED BEANS

2 cups dried beans
½ pound scored salt pork
1 tablespoon chopped onion
1 teaspoon ground ginger
½ cup honey
1 teaspoon salt
1 teaspoon dry mustard

Soak washed beans in 4 cups warm water 3 hours.

Cook on low heat in tightly covered saucepan 1¼ hours. Do not allow to boil. Drain the beans, saving the water.

Place salt pork in the bottom of bean pot and add beans. Cover with mixture made of the bean water, onion, ginger, honey, salt, and mustard. Add boiling water, if needed. Place small pieces of salt pork on top, cover pot, and bake in slow oven about 6 hours. Uncover bean pot during last hour of baking. If the beans become too dry, add a little boiling water.

FAVORITE CANDIED YAMS

1½ cups honey
2 tablespoons cornstarch
⅛ teaspoon salt
1½ cups water
1 tablespoon butter
6 large yams, sliced and cooked

Mix and cook all ingredients, except yams, until mixture is clear. Pour over cooked sweet potatoes and bake at 400° until brown. Also very good over baked apples.

FLUFFY SWEET POTATO CASSEROLE

6 medium-sized sweet potatoes
¼ cup butter
¼ cup brown sugar, firmly packed
¼ cup honey
1 tablespoon grated orange rind
½ teaspoon salt
½ cup chopped pecans
Marshmallows
Orange sections

Cook sweet potatoes in boiling water until tender, drain, and mash. Combine mashed sweet potatoes with butter, brown sugar, honey, grated orange rind, and salt; fold in pecans and mix well. Pile mixture in baking casserole which has been greased with shortening or butter. Garnish with marshmallows and orange sections. Bake at 350° for 30–35 minutes or until thoroughly heated.

SALADS AND DRESSINGS

BANANA-NUT AMBROSIA

2 bananas, cut crosswise
4 maraschino cherries, cut in half
Lettuce leaves
¼ cup mayonnaise
2 tablespoons honey
1 tablespoon pineapple juice
¼ cup chopped nuts
¼ cup shredded coconut

Arrange sliced bananas and cherries on greens. Mix mayonnaise, honey, and juice; spoon over fruit. Sprinkle nuts and coconut on top.

HONEY CABBAGE SALAD

1 medium head cabbage, shredded
1 medium cantaloupe
5 canned pear halves in syrup
Strawberries and mint leaves

HONEY SOY DRESSING:

½ cup fresh lemon juice
⅓ cup honey
½ teaspoon grated lemon rind
1 drop mint extract
½ cup oil
2 tablespoons toasted sesame seeds
1 teaspoon chutney
½ teaspoon soy sauce
Dash of salt

Shred cabbage and crisp in ice water for 10 minutes. Drain and dry thoroughly.

Add a drop of mint extract and green coloring to pear syrup. Let the pear halves absorb the color and flavor.

Remove rind and seeds of the cantaloupe. Save one half for cutting into slices for garnish. Cut the remainder into ½" cubes.

Prepare the Honey Soy Dressing by shaking ingredients together in a covered jar. Chill. Toss cabbage and cantaloupe cubes with Honey Soy Dressing. Garnish with cantaloupe slices, pear halves, strawberries, and mint leaves.

PINK SHRIMP-ORANGE SALAD

3 medium oranges, peeled, cut into bite-size pieces (1½ cups)
½ cup sliced celery
½ cup sliced ripe olives
½ pound cleaned, cooked shrimp
2 tablespoons chopped onion
¼ teaspoon salt
Lettuce

CITRUS HONEY DRESSING:

¼ cup honey
½ cup mayonnaise
1 tablespoon grated orange peel
3 tablespoons fresh orange juice
1 tablespoon fresh lemon juice
½ teaspoon paprika

Combine orange pieces, celery, olives, shrimp, chopped onion, and salt.

To make Citrus Honey Dressing, combine all ingredients and blend well.

To the shrimp mixture, add a little Citrus Honey Dressing to moisten. Chill. Serve in lettuce cup on individual salad plates with Citrus Honey Dressing.

AVOCADO AND FRUIT SALAD

1 avocado, chilled and peeled
2 grapefruits, chilled, peeled, and
   sectioned
2–3 oranges, chilled, peeled, and
   sectioned
Lettuce
Watercress, ripe olives for garnish

Cut avocado in half crosswise, remove seed, slice into thin circles; cut each circle in half. On individual lettuce-lined salad plates alternately arrange grapefruit and avocado sections, rounded edges up. Place orange sections around other fruits. Garnish with watercress and ripe olives. Serve with Honey French Dressing (below).

PEAR SUNSHINE TRAY

5 canned Bartlett pear halves
5 canned Freestone peach halves
5 stuffed dates
5 walnut halves
1 grapefruit, sectioned
1 red apple
Grapes, sliced
Salad greens, torn

HONEY FRENCH DRESSING:

¼ cup honey
¼ cup lemon juice
¼ cup salad oil
½ cup pear juice
Few grains salt
½ teaspoon celery seed
¼ teaspoon dry mustard

Drain juice from the can of pears. Arrange fruits on a bed of crisp salad greens with stuffed dates atop the peach halves.

Prepare Honey French Dressing by combining all ingredients in a jar and shake until well blended. Serve over fruit tray.

WALNUT JEWEL SALAD

3-ounce package pineapple-flavored
   gelatin
1 cup hot water
½ teaspoon salt
1 cup cold liquid (drained pineapple
   juice plus water)
1 cup chopped raw cranberries
½ cup canned crushed pineapple,
   drained
½ cup diced celery
½ cup chopped walnuts

HONEY CREME SALAD DRESSING:

3-ounce package cream cheese
¼ teaspoon salt
2 tablespoons honey
¼ cup sour cream

Dissolve gelatin in hot water. Add salt and cold water/drained-pineapple juice mixture. Chill until slightly thickened. Fold in remaining ingredients. Turn into a one-quart mold or into eight individual molds. Chill until firm. Unmold onto bed of crisp lettuce, and decorate with additional walnuts.

To prepare Honey Creme Salad Dressing, whip or mash cream cheese in a small bowl with salt, honey, and sour cream. Serve over salad.

HONEY-GLAZED ORANGE SLICES

¼ cup honey
¼ teaspoon nutmeg (optional)
2 tablespoons butter or margarine
8 orange slices, ¼" thick
Whole cloves

Blend honey, butter, and nutmeg in a skillet until butter is melted. Stud orange rind with cloves. Simmer orange slices in honey. Glaze 15 minutes. Turn frequently to glaze evenly. Delicious served with roast duckling.

HONEY CRANBERRY RELISH

2 cups fresh cranberries
1 orange
1 cup honey

Sort and wash cranberries. Wash and quarter orange. Put orange and cranberries through food chopper. Add honey and mix well. Let stand overnight. Chill before serving.

BANANA FRUIT DRESSING

1 ripe banana, mashed
3 tablespoons honey
¼ cup orange juice
¼ teaspoon salt
½ cup buttermilk

Combine banana, honey, orange juice, and salt; gradually stir in buttermilk. Whip with a rotary beater until smooth. Chill. Serve with fresh fruit salad.

HONEY CHEESE DRESSING

½ cup cottage cheese
2 tablespoons honey
1 teaspoon grated lemon rind
1¼ tablespoons lemon juice
½ teaspoon salt
½ cup salad oil

Force cottage cheese through sieve, add honey, lemon rind and juice, and salt; beat briskly with egg beater. Add oil, a teaspoon at a time, until half the oil is used, blending well between each addition. Add remaining oil 2 tablespoons at a time.

A delicious dressing for fruit salads or avocados.

HONEY OF A DRESSING

Add ¼ cup honey to ¾ cup sour cream. Mix gently and thoroughly.

FRUIT FRENCH DRESSING

⅓ cup honey
1 teaspoon salt
1 teaspoon paprika
1 cup unsweetened pineapple juice
2 well-beaten eggs
6 ounces cream cheese
¼ cup orange juice
2½ tablespoons lemon juice

Mix dry ingredients, add honey and fruit juices, and blend. Cook in double boiler 20 minutes, stirring constantly. Slowly stir into eggs. Cook 5 minutes, stirring constantly. Cool slightly. Soften cream cheese; beat into cooked mixture. Chill.

POPPY SEED SALAD DRESSING

⅓ cup strained honey
½ teaspoon salt
⅓ cup vinegar
3 tablespoons prepared mustard
1¼ cups salad oil
2½ tablespoons poppy seeds

Mix ingredients together in the order given. Blend with an electric blender or mixer until smooth.

CREAMY HONEY DRESSING

3 ounces cream cheese
⅓ cup cider vinegar
¼ cup honey
½ teaspoon cinnamon
1 teaspoon paprika
1 teaspoon salt
¼ cup salad oil

Blend cream cheese and vinegar. Add honey and seasonings. Mix well and whip in salad oil.

HONEY LIME DRESSING

6 ounces frozen limeade concentrate
¾ cup salad oil
½ cup honey
¼ teaspoon salt
2 teaspoons celery seed

Put limeade, salad oil, honey, and salt in a blender container. Blend a few seconds. Stir in celery seed. (Mixture may be beaten or shaken to mix.) Serve over fresh or canned fruit salad.

HONEY DRESSING

⅔ cup sugar
1 teaspoon dry mustard
1 teaspoon paprika
1 teaspoon celery seed
¼ teaspoon salt
⅓ cup strained honey
5 tablespoons vinegar
1 tablespoon lemon juice
1 teaspoon grated onion
1 cup salad oil

Mix dry ingredients. Add honey, vinegar, lemon juice, and onion. Pour oil into mixture very slowly, beating constantly with rotary or electric beater or in blender.

LEMON-LIME DRESSING

2 eggs, beaten
¼ cup lemon juice
¼ cup lime juice
⅔ cup honey
½ teaspoon salt
1 tablespoon snipped chives or parsley
1 cup sour cream

Mix eggs, juices, and honey in little saucepan. Stir over low heat until thickened. Let cool a bit. Mix remaining ingredients, then fold into egg mixture. Chill.

INDEX OF RECIPES

DESSERTS AND DESSERT SAUCES